James De Borley

PIONEERS' SCRAPBOOK

PIONEERS' SCRAPBOOK

REMINISCENCES OF KENYA 1890 TO 1968

EDITED BY ELSPETH HUXLEY AND ARNOLD CURTIS

FOREWORD BY H R H PRINCESS ALICE, DUCHESS OF GLOUCESTER

Evans

EVANS BROTHERS LIMITED
LONDON

Published by Evans Brothers Limited
Montague House, Russell Square,
London WC1B 5BX

Evans Brothers (Nigeria Publishers)
Limited
PMB5164, Jericho Road,
Ibadan

First published 1980

Cartoons by ffolkes

Filmset in 12 point Photina
and printed by
BAS Printers Limited,
Over Wallop, Hampshire

ISBN 0 237 50560 6   PRA 7016

CONTENTS

Page

Introduction 7

Acknowledgements 10

Foreword 11

1 Nairobi and its Neighbourhood 13

2 Limuru 29

3 Kiambu and Ruiru 35

4 Kikuyu and Muguga 43

5 Thika 51

6 Makuyu and Mitubiri 57

7 Naivasha, Gilgil and the Kinangop 61

8 Nakuru 69

9 Subukia and Solai 77

10 Londiani and Mau Summit 87

11 Molo and Turi 93

12 Eldoret and its Neighbourhood 97

13 Trans Nzoia 107

14 Kisumu 117

15 Machakos and Ulu 119

16 Mombasa 129

17 Laikipia 137

18 Nyeri 143

19 Nanyuki 149

Glossary 156

Index 157

INTRODUCTION

In December 1963 the Union Jack was hauled down in Nairobi and the independent Republic of Kenya was born. The colonial period had lasted less than 70 years. When a British Protectorate was declared in 1895, the East African interior was occupied by peoples whose way of life had changed little for centuries. Some, nomads like the Maasai, herded their hump-backed cattle over enormous plains which they shared with the greatest concourse of wild animals the world has ever seen. Others cleared areas of bush, and burned clearings in forests in order to grow their plots of beans and millet, and herd their goats. There were neither roads, nor towns; no kingdoms or principalities such as existed in other parts of Africa; no carts or wagons for transport, only the backs of women or donkeys; no ploughs, only digging-sticks. Skins were these peoples' clothing; beads or shells were their currency; herbs and spells were their medicines; the art of writing was unknown.

In stressing the apparent simplicity of life in this part of pre-colonial Africa, I am not trying to denigrate it. As technology advances, life in our western urban and materialist societies seems to many less and less attractive, and life in technologically simpler societies appears by contrast to have human virtues which our own world increasingly ignores and denies. I am merely suggesting how East Africa looked to the first white people to cross the uninhabited, arid bushlands between the coast, with its old Arab seaports, and the highlands with their great rolling downlands and forests, their high mountains and deep valleys, their lakes and rivers and apparent emptiness.

The first white settlers came to the East Africa Protectorate, as it was then known, because of the railway. This single-track 'lunatic line', as *Punch* called it, was built at what was then considered to be enormous expense from Mombasa on the Indian Ocean to the shores of Lake Victoria, with the main purposes of succouring missionaries who had already established themselves inland, and 'opening up' the country to outside influences which, it was believed, would complete the suppression of the Arab-conducted slave trade. This trade, which had ravaged much of East and Central Africa, was already on the decline, but it still continued, and the best way to end it was considered to be (as Livingstone had urged) to plant and foster permanent settlements of Europeans. There was an additional aim of ending tribal wars and substituting the *Pax Britannica*, then thought to be a 'good thing'.

The railway reached its terminus in 1901 — but how could it be made to pay its way? Apart from supplies for the few missions and government posts in the interior, there was nothing for it to carry in, and even less to carry out. When Africans cultivated the land, they did so only to feed themselves and barter with each other what little surplus might arise. Here were these great expanses of fertile land lying idle, so far as the outside world was concerned; and the outside world, with its expanding populations, was hungry for the crops that might be made to flourish there with the aid of European expertise. The decision was made to invite Europeans to take up uninhabited and uncultivated land believed at the time, not always correctly, to belong to nobody. Land in current tribal occupation was set aside as 'native reserves' where newcomers were not allowed to buy or lease farms. So, at the beginning of the twentieth century (a few individuals had arrived before) the first contingent of white settlers was allocated blocks of land on long leases from the Protectorate Government.

Naturally their womenfolk came too, and set up homes, often little more elaborate than the round thatched huts of the Africans, amid bush and forest and on the veld. Gradually, roads (of a sort) were made, small townships developed, and district associations formed to discuss the problems and promote the interests of the local white farmers. Districts varied widely in their nature, in the kind of crops and livestock they were fitted for, and in their atmosphere; and, surprisingly soon, local loyalties grew up towards the various districts in which white families had established their homes. Machakos was quite different from Nanyuki, Kiambu from Timau, and so on. Agricultural shows, started very early in the Colony's history, fostered these local loyalties. Displays of home-grown produce and home industries, organized and run by the women, competed for prizes, and a keen spirit of inter-district competition was kindled which led on to welfare and community work.

In 1917, the East Africa Women's League was started by a group of activists in the field of welfare among all races. By no means all the members were drawn from farms; the business community, government officials' wives, and people from the railway and other services were involved. The main objects were twofold. The short-term one, soon achieved, was to secure votes for women at elections to the Colony's Legislative Council; the long-term one, so long-term as to be perpetual, was 'to take an interest in, and action on where necessary, all matters affecting the welfare and happiness of women and children of all races'. The words 'of all races' were important; from the first, although the membership was European, welfare among African women and children was a major concern of the League. The various district branches were its foundation, and gave it durability and strength.

In 1967 the League celebrated its Golden Jubilee. To mark the occasion, each of its branches was invited to prepare a scrapbook. Into these went, as the name implies, all manner of things—childhood recollections by Kenya-born men and women, reaching back to pioneer days; old newspaper cuttings; notes on flora and fauna; everything from rainfall statistics to tall stories involving lions, from encounters with pythons and baboons to the classification of dhows. There was also a profusion of photographs. It seemed to the Council of the League that these scrapbooks held too much material of historical and general interest to remain locked away in their archives, and so a much condensed version was prepared for publication: here it is.

This assemblage of snapshots, both photographic and verbal, of life in the East Africa Protectorate, which had become Kenya in 1920, does not pretend to offer serious historical studies of the early colonial period. Politics have been rigidly eschewed. Its concern is with side-shows rather than events in the central arena, with the small events of daily life, the things that have stuck in peoples' minds. Though by no means all the contributions have come from women, a good many have, and I think this gives them a particular interest. Since the aim of most settlers is sooner or later to establish a home, and since homes are made mainly by women, it is obvious that feminine experiences and viewpoints are worth attention, yet they are seldom recorded. The reasons are equally obvious. Most women, at least those on farms, are too busy to leave records, and most history is written by men. But in these pages women have their say.

Only a very small proportion of the material in the 22 district scrap-books has been selected, but enough, I hope, to give something of the flavour of those bygone days—the hopes and the excitements, the triumphs and disasters, the humour, above all the gaiety and courage that kept the early settlers battling on through endless-seeming droughts, plagues of locusts, fires and floods, collapsed markets, and the personal tragedies frequent in countries where there is no doctor round the corner and no policeman in his radio-linked patrol car cruising by.

Readers may like to know what has become of the East Africa Women's League. Many people thought that after Kenya's Independence a body that had been so closely bound up with the settler community would fade away. Its vitality confounded these prophecies. Adapting itself to the times, the League widened its membership but maintained its aims. In the United Kingdom there is now a flourishing branch whose members have left Kenya behind but who still follow the country's fortunes with interest and affection; and in the League's country of origin the tradition established by its founders of voluntary service to the community is being faithfully carried on by a new generation of Kenyan citizens.

Elspeth Huxley
1979

ACKNOWLEDGEMENTS

The members of the East African Women's League and their friends who contributed prose, verse or pictures to the various district scrapbooks have allowed the league to reproduce their work, if desired, in book form. We wish to record our thanks to them.

We also wish to record our thanks to the 'Standard', formerly the 'East African Standard' for permission to reproduce the following:

Page 106 A boran bull at Kaluptui 22 March 1968
Page 114 Mzee Jomo Kenyatta at Kitale Show 4 November 1968
Page 131 Fort Jesus and Mombasa Club from the air February 1964
Page 155 The opening of Secret Valley 'Charging rhino maroons Governor' 18 August 1961

Page 57 We acknowledge Camera Press for this picture of Mount Kenya

Although we have done our best to trace the owners of copyright material in order to obtain permission to reproduce we think that there could still be a few instances where copyright may have infringed. If there are such copyright owners whose works have inadvertently been reproduced without permission we hope that they will accept our apologies. We should also welcome information on such cases so that the matter may be put right in any subsequent edition of this book.

FOREWORD

In writing this foreword, I would like to say how glad I am that the East Africa Women's League has decided to recall these early memories of those pioneers who, for one reason or another, decided to risk their future by starting life anew in what was then thought of as 'darkest Africa'.

To venture into such an unknown country needed courage, endurance and ability to deal with any kind of unexpected circumstance, and plans that so often failed a first, second or even third time. When reading these recollections, it will be apparent that such hardships were more than compensated for by the sunshine, the colourful scenery, the wild life all around; the soothing sound of crickets and bull frogs as darkness fell, and the variety of animal voices in the forest at night.

Fifty years have passed since I first knew Kenya and much has changed since then, but those who read this book will share with me happy memories of early days recorded therein, thus ensuring they will now not be forgotten.

Kenya must surely have benefited somewhat from the lives and example of many who, with the best intentions, tried to show as well as they could their own way of life to all those who were to follow and rule the destinies of this most beautiful part of all Africa.

Alice

HRH Princess Alice, Duchess of Gloucester
Patron of the East Africa Women's League

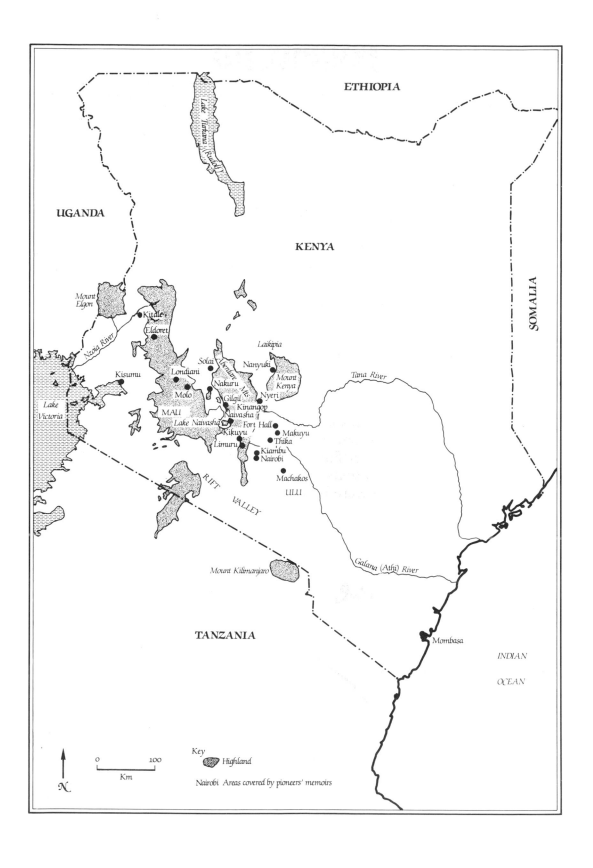

ETHIOPIA

KENYA

UGANDA

SOMALIA

Lake Turkana (Rudolf)

Mount
Elgon

Kitale
Eldoret

Nzoia River

Laikipia

Solai   Nanyuki
Kisumu   Londiani   Nakuru   Mount
Molo   Gilgil   Kenya
Lake   MAU   Kinangop   Nyeri
Victoria   Lake Naivasha   Naivasha
Kikuyu   Fort Hall
Limuru   Makuyu
Kiambu   Thika
Nairobi

Machakos

ULU

Tana River

Galana (Athi) River

RIFT   VALLEY

Mount Kilimanjaro

TANZANIA

Mombasa

INDIAN

OCEAN

N

0   100

Km

Key   🞄 Highland

Nairobi Areas covered by pioneers' memoirs

ONE
NAIROBI AND ITS NEIGHBOURHOOD

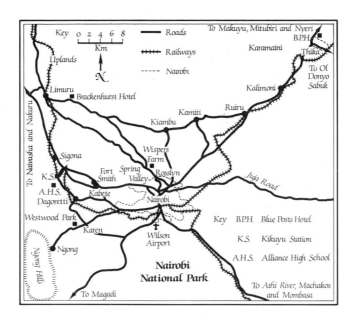

Fort Smith

Fort Smith, a few miles north-west of Nairobi, was built in 1892 by the Imperial British East Africa Company. It had a stockade 250 feet wide surrounded by a deep ditch, and contained the first brick house in East Africa, made from local clay. Major Eric Smith was the designer and first commandant.

For a time the fort was practically besieged by the Kikuyu, but in 1897 Chief Kinyanjui and Captain Francis Hall (founder of Fort Hall) each planted a *mugumu* branch (wild fig) which, being bound together, grew in unity as a symbol of peace between Britain and the Kikuyu.

At the end of 1896 Doctor and Mrs Boedeker arrived at Fort Smith after a march from the coast. Mrs Lesley Williams (née Boedeker) describes the scene from her father's diary:

'My father and mother were welcomed by Mr Hall and his assistant Mr Lane. Watched by a large crowd of Africans the caravan arrived after a long, weary journey of six weeks, headed by my parents, who were followed by a long line of porters singing and beating drums. The cool climate and lovely countryside soon made up for all the hardships endured since leaving England. Father brought the first mouldboard plough into Kenya. In anticipation of the arrival of this rare implement Mr Hall had trained some oxen, and the team went into action watched by a large crowd, which included Chief Kinyanjui. When the people saw

*Mrs Helen Boedeker
at Fort Smith in
1897 taken shortly
after a six week walk
from Mombasa*

the earth being turned over by the oxen, as it appeared to them, they roared with laughter.'

Household goods must have come later, since a note of her mother's records: 'Mr Hall has lent me a *sufuria* – a little beauty with a cast iron lid in which I can make cakes nicely.'

The diary also records the shooting of a man-eating lioness on the site of Nairobi, by Corporal Ellis, 'who then took snaps'. Corporal, later Sergeant, Ellis was Nairobi's first European resident. The street called after him in the city centre has been re-named City Hall Way.

On 22 June 1897 Fort Smith celebrated Queen Victoria's Diamond Jubilee. A Captain Dugmore played the organ – one wonders how this reached Fort Smith – and Dr Boedeker the violin.

The Hill

Kenya's capital was the offspring of the Uganda Railway, as it was then called. Starting from Mombasa in May 1896, almost exactly three years later the platelayers reached Mile 327, a spot described by R O Preston as 'a bleak, swampy stretch of soppy landscape, devoid of human habitation of any sort, the resort of thousands of wild animals of every species'; he added that 'it did not boast a single tree'. It did however boast a little stream, called by the Maasai Uaso Nairobi (cold water), beside which Sergeant Ellis of the Royal Engineers had already formed a small transport depot with mules and oxen. Here a temporary railhead was established while the engineers tackled the steep, difficult climb into the highlands ahead.

Before the end of 1899 George Whitehouse, the Chief Engineer, had moved from Mombasa with most of his staff to this bleak but invigorating camp, and to it the railway workshops were transferred. His was the first house to be built on a rise above the river, which became known as Railway Hill. By 1901 there were enough Europeans to form the Railway Club, whose present building was put up in 1912.

So, year by year, Nairobi spread, at first a sprawl of wooden bungalows with corrugated iron roofs, and shacks made of old paraffin tins. Asian traders established a bazaar. Kikuyu women brought in produce and a market sprang up. In 1902 bubonic plague broke out and the Principal Medical Officer had the whole place burnt down. The shanty-town soon sprang up again and continued to grow: ramshackle, higgledy-piggledy, flooded in the rainy season and dust-enshrouded in the dry.

By 1905 the Norfolk Hotel was under construction, and Mrs Elliot had a tiny tea-room where she sold her home-baked cakes and bread. (This became Elliot's Bakery.) Today's prosperous suburb of Spring Valley was then a single 'farm', i.e. stretch of untouched Africa, leased to Messrs Evans and Langmore.

The first stone house built in Nairobi still stands, near the Ambassadeur Hotel. It belonged to Mrs Cowie. In 1905 she left it for the wilds of Parklands, where all

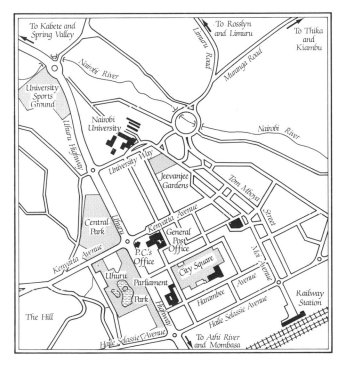

Nairobi today

kinds of game, particularly wild pig, strayed out of the forest into her garden.

The settlers of 1905 favoured a Wild West kind of apparel: ten-gallon hats, bright shirts, and belts supporting a revolver. A little culture began to raise its head with smoking concerts and garden fêtes, and even a Promenade Concert was organized by a few enthusiastic amateurs and held above the Ainsworth Bridge. The Duke and Duchess of Connaught came out to unveil a statue of Queen Victoria – the one presented by Mr Jeevanjee – which now stands in the Jeevanjee Gardens.

Flags were flown from the Post Office in Sixth Avenue to indicate the movement of mail. A blue flag meant that a ship had left Aden for Mombasa bearing mail. A red flag meant that overseas mail had been received. A white flag, or white arc lamp at night, showed that the mail was ready for distribution.

In 1905 Ainsworth Bridge was washed away twice in one week by the heavy rains. An early meeting of the Town Council decided that roads in the commercial areas should be called Streets, those in the Hill district Avenues, those in Parklands Drives, and those in the Asian areas simply Roads. Oil lamps were the earliest form of street lighting. There was often a public outcry when they were shot out with a revolver by a marksman in a passing rickshaw.

It is clear that early Nairobi was regarded as by no means a place of beauty nor a health resort. Winston Churchill saw it in 1907 and described it as being 'in an unhealthy situation, low and swampy with an indifferent water supply'.

Recollections

by Grace Udall (Mrs Wilkinson)

When we came to East Africa in 1908 we were rowed ashore in little boats from our ship, then we scrambled with our luggage on to trolleys which were pushed along the track by Africans, singing on the downhill stretches and puffing and grunting on the uphill bits. Thus we arrived in Mombasa.

In the train we found ourselves covered in layers and layers of red dust as we slowly chugged our way up country, climbing steadily as the engine gobbled up tons and tons of wood fuel.

It seemed as if the whole of Nairobi had come to the station to meet the train. The hustle and bustle of white-robed people shouting at the tops of their voices, the rickshaw men grabbing your luggage and making off with it, the great Ali Khan with his riding boots and long whip there to take Government officials in his open wagon drawn by a span of mules – all this made a colourful and exciting stage in our journey. We hired two rickshaws and trotted off along the dirt road, with huge gum trees on either side, also a few corrugated iron buildings, and more than a few ruts in the way. This was Government Road (now Moi Avenue). After what seemed hours we arrived at our new home in Second Avenue, Parklands, a small corrugated iron house on stilts. Three Africans greeted us, and so began our life in a new and raw land.

When we went to visit friends for afternoon tea, my brother and I were dressed

Government Road from Market, Nairobi

Bottom: an early photograph of Sixth Avenue, later Delamere Avenue, now Kenyatta Avenue

up in white starched cotton with lace edging. Off we set, often with the sun blazing straight into our eyes, and as we grew hotter and hotter we dripped all over our beautiful white dresses. The rickshaw men were dressed up too in their 'livery'. Each household vied with the next in rigging out its rickshaw team.

My father had a bicycle, and when the telephone failed between Nairobi and Ruiru he would set off at night to cycle the 20 miles there and back, with several papyrus swamps on the way, where hippos and crocodiles wandered across the road. Once, when he got to Ruiru, he found the water no longer running into the power station; a hippo had been sucked broadside across the grille above the intake and got stuck. Eventually it had to be shot, and then a long wait occurred until it became bloated and so water-borne, and was ignominiously towed away.

One year the rains were long and heavy and the roads got worse and worse. Government Road in particular had great potholes in it. The Public Works Department set to work to repair it, digging up long stretches. Then they disappeared, and the road became almost impassable. My father and several other citizens went into the town one night and under cover of darkness planted the road up with banana trees, cabbages and sugar-cane, to the amusement of all next morning. The PWD came and repaired the road soon after.

A colourful ceremony which took place in those early days was the weighing of the Aga Khan in gold at the Aga Khan Club opposite the City Park. Everyone wore gorgeous saris and turbans. The Aga Khan, a portly gentleman, sat on a huge weighing scale, and bars of gold were added on the opposite side until very slowly the scale lifted him off the ground, when a big cheer went up. I remember dancing at the ball held in the evening, where the Begum wore a sari with real diamonds scattered over it.

The City Park, which was beautifully laid out with flowering trees and plants and green lawns, was formally opened by the Duke and Duchess of York, who were on a visit to Nairobi, while my father was Mayor. It was a great day.

Spring Valley birds

by Elizabeth Drews

We have a bird table outside our window and to this come little African Fire Finches, Streaky Seed-Eaters, and the tiny Bronze Mannikins eagerly seeking millet seed. There is one lone Black Finch who never seems to have a mate, but his appetite is not impaired. If bread is on offer a noisy gang of Grey Headed Sparrows and bright Yellow Weavers descend from the electric wire near by. An avocado pear sometimes tempts Bulbuls and Olive Thrushes, but these are shyer birds and they are content to stay under the trees and eat their fruit there.

The Bronzy Sunbird and his wife build a nest in a different tree each year and line it with the soft fawn wool that I brush from our Alsatian. The little Red Finches prefer feathers from the chicken run, and it is not unusual to watch a little cock bird with a feather as big as himself spend several minutes trying to gain sufficient height to fly over the hedge. This year we seem to have had more than our share of the Rainbird, and this Red-Chested Cuckoo can really get on one's nerves with its 'it will rain' call. The Bellbird, too, is frequently heard.

One year a pair of Striped Swallows decided to build in our verandah. They made their tiny mud pellets from the puddles and then darted in to fix them firmly in the selected spot. We were sorry that they only hatched one baby, and on returning the following year were ousted by a pair of Martins. The Red-eyed Dove and Laughing Dove both frequent our garden, and the dog becomes neurotic trying to creep up on them as they forage on the lawn. They wait until the last moment and then fly up under his nose. A pair of hawks has lived in the Gilbert Road valley for many years and these wheel over the district looking for food. They took a month-old chicken from our lawn, and once I saw a frustrated bird dive down on an old tennis ball, but fail to lift it. The Spotted Eagle Owl nests in the vicinity and many a night I wake to hear its mournful hooting, an eerie sound in the dead of night.

Of course I have not mentioned all the birds we see. The little grey White-eyed Flycatchers eat our mulberries, and the Shrikes with their spotless black and white plumage sit in the Bauhinia trees. Robin Chats are rather rare, but like the fallen avocado pears lying under the tree. Weavers hang their fantastic nests from several trees and my son and I once tried to copy one. How they managed to do such intricate weaving with a beak and a few claws was quite beyond us, and soon we gave up trying. In the meantime I note our banana leaves are in ribbons so I guess they are at it again. Once we went to investigate what sounded like barking puppies in the garden only to find that it was a pair of Turacoes in the Bombax tree.

Masara, built in 1906, picture taken in about 1914

Masara

by Margaret Elkington

We arrived from England in about July 1905, and were taken to the Norfolk Hotel by Major J. H. Gailey, founder of the engineering firm, Gailey and Roberts. Major Gailey had come to work on the Railway and once, when he had been out of a job, he and a companion had sung themselves across South America, singing English music-hall songs.

There were only two houses to let and we took the one in Spring Valley, which belonged to Mr Langmore and Mr Evans. Ours was an unlined tin bungalow with three rooms, an earth floor, and a few cane chairs and tables. The kitchen was a lean-to with three stones to cook on. We had to undress on our camp beds because of the rats.

In 1906 this country was all open grassland with very few trees. We sat on our verandah in the evening and saw the lights of trains coming across the Athi Plains. We could see both Mount Kenya and Mount Kilimanjaro, and the Ngong Hills. Racing had already started, so Father (Jim Elkington) built stables and became a very successful trainer. We used to ride down to the old Nairobi Racecourse to work the horses in the early mornings, six miles. Mr Goldfinch had a small pack of imported foxhounds which he gave to us, and they were the foundation of the Masara Hunt. We imported more foxhounds from Lord Leconfield and by 1912 had 30 couples.

We built Masara in 1906: three rooms with an eight-foot verandah all round the ends, the back of which was divided into smaller rooms.

By 1908 we had 5000 coffee trees.

Kabete

The first Europeans to establish themselves in the Kabete district, north-west of Nairobi, were members of the Church Missionary Society, who opened a Mission in 1900 on land bought from Chege, Mrs Josiah Njonjo's father, for 50 goats. Canon and Mrs Leakey (he was then the Rev. Harry Leakey) arrived there in 1902 with their two baby daughters, travelling on foot and by hammock from Kikuyu Station, six miles away. Their first home was a mud and thatch hut, but a stone house was built in 1906. The late Dr Louis Leakey, the anthropologist, was born there, and also his brother, Douglas, formerly of the Forestry Department.

In 1904 Canon Leakey took 12 boys into a Mission hut to be educated. One of them was to become Chief Josiah Njonjo, the father of our present Attorney-General. Another was Paul Likimani, the first Maasai to seek education after working for Lord Delamere at Gilgil. He was the father of Dr Jason Likimani, former Director of Medical Services.

Canon Leakey planted strawberries at Kabete and put sticks to hold netting over them. Those sticks grew into large *mugumu* trees and can still be seen at the Mary Leakey Girls' School.

The Coopers of Kirawa

by Jim Cooper

My uncle, Archie Cooper, went to BEA in 1896 as assistant accountant to the Uganda Railway. In 1904 he suggested to my father, Douglas Cooper, that he should take up land in partnership with himself, two Harrison cousins and J H

Gailey. The immediate object was to grow potatoes for the South African market. Their capital was £500 and a lot of hope.

Archie had spent his younger days in South America, and after the first war became General Manager of the Peruvian Railways. C N M Harrison was a lawyer and founder partner of the Nairobi law firm. His cousin, Edgar, was a cowboy in Texas before getting a commission in the Duke of Wellington's Regiment. He was seconded to the Sultan of Zanzibar's army in 1896 and took part in the Arab Revolt and the Uganda Mutiny. Amongst other exploits he marched from Machakos to Jinja (Uganda) in 21 days with his company, fighting an action at Ravine and at Mumias on the way. He was awarded a CB and DSO for his services. My father had spent his twenties in Chile. The land they took up at Kabete was 3000 acres, stretching from the railway line, where Wellcome Institute now is, to Matundu Estate and Kitisuru. Archie named it Kirawa.

I remember listening to a story told by an old Kikuyu called Waweru who held his audience spellbound one evening as we were waiting for the carts to return to collect coffee from the shamba. He was describing a raid carried out by Maasai from Ngong. They raided up where the CMS Mission was later established. The Kikuyu moran circled round behind the Maasai and ambushed them on their return on the ridge where Kirime Kimwe Estate now lies. The Maasai were killed and the women who were carrying the spoils of the raid, mostly food from the shamba, had their right hands cut off. This was the year of the Great Famine, 1897. When Kirime Kimwe was being ploughed up after the First War for planting coffee, I can remember, as a small boy, the ploughmen placing skulls on sticks to act as markers – something a small boy remembers vividly.

Rosslyn

Rosslyn today is a smart little suburb, attractively laid out with well-built houses set in pretty gardens, each with about five acres, some with more. The residents, who mostly work in Nairobi, are still allowed to keep horses or cows.

The first land sale on record is a Homestead Agreement, as it was then called, between the Crown and Terence Mabert in 1904. In 1905 the Crown sold land to T A Wood, later Mayor of Nairobi, and to Newton Wilson, whose holding became (1928) the Rosslyn Estate owned by Prince William of Sweden, Mr Bildt and Mr Forsby. The manager was Jack Tate, whose sister-in-law started the old Stanley Hotel in Victoria (now Tom Mboya) Street. This did so well that they decided to expand, and Jack Tate attended an auction of plots. He had a total of £305 in the world, but the opposition had bid up to £305. Legend has it that he called out: 'Anyone lend me a fiver?' and a voice from the crowd said: 'I will, old friend'. So Tate bid £310 and thus obtained the site of the present New Stanley Hotel.

Until the thirties the Rosslyn area was all farms carved out of bush and forest, with cart-tracks for roads, and conditions were hard and primitive. Malaria, tick typhus and typhoid were common, and there were no adequate drugs. Everyone wore topees or double felt hats with broad brims, with long sleeves and long trousers, or skirts, to protect them from the sun. Normally no one worked out of doors between 11.30 a.m. and 4 p.m. It was considered dangerous to get too much sun, and unhealthy for women to stay here longer than a year at a stretch. Parents were advised to send daughters home after the age of nine, as they 'developed too fast'. As a result of all this most of the children looked white and pasty with dark rings under their eyes. A Mrs Day was said to have got sunstroke through the knees. She was out all day in the normal khaki jacket with padded spinepad and a topee, but with this outfit she wore shorts, which proved to be her downfall. She had to leave the country for good.

In Nairobi there was Dr Burkitt, a doctor with some peculiar ideas. His treatment for malaria was to wrap his patient in a wet sheet and take him for a drive in his open Ford car, to get his temperature down. On one occasion he is said to have travelled miles to some lonely farm to pick up an old woman who was very ill. He put her in the back of his car and set off for the hospital. On the way he saw a magnificent lion – too good a trophy to miss. He took a quick look at his passenger dozing in the back of the car, gave her a shot of morphia, got out and shot his lion and put it in the back beside the old girl. When he arrived at the hospital he forgot about the lion and dashed in to tell the matron that the patient had arrived. She went out and opened the door of the car and the lion fell at her feet. At any rate, that is the story.

The Watkins of Wispers Farm

by Veronica Hughes

The year was 1923 and it was pouring with rain when Oscar and Olga Watkins, my father and mother, bought Wispers from Newton Wilson.

The old house on stilts was so filthy that Olga decided to abandon it and start again elsewhere. That is where we are now. There was no money so Olga cut *sanji* grass and sold it; this enabled her to employ a Seychellois mason. He was a marvellous man who could turn his hand to anything. She then advertised that she would undertake 'any building job that no one else would do'. As a result most of her commissions were for long drops, i.e. earth latrines. Her clients would come to Wispers to be shown a selection and quoted prices. Those with stable doors and well sited for a view cost a little more. On one occasion she pointed to our own 'little house' and said: 'Well, you can have that just as it stands for £5.' Whereupon my father's voice from within said: 'Thanks'. He always spoke of this as the occasion when his wife sold him for £5 thrown in with a long drop.

At this time we lived in two mud huts while the house was being built. The bricks and tiles were all made locally by the brickworks next door, which was started about 1914 by Tom Young and his wife, a charming Kentish couple of the old variety. There was no road to Wispers and this was the first task, entailing quite a bit of blasting and many narrow squeaks. A bridge had to be made over the Karura River, and another over the swamp near what is now the Shell Sports

Top: mowing the lawn at Wispers, 1927
Bottom: Oscar and Olga Watkins shopping in the middle of Nairobi, 1915

Club. Olga then set to work to plant coffee. She ploughed 100 acres herself, driving the team of 16 oxen. And so Wispers became a family home, where we had at one time 16 dogs and 23 cats, all but two of these picked up as starving strays. We had a bulldog, a leopard, a tame cock, a Kavirondo Crane, two horses, and the donkey who brought our water up from the river. Olga always had room for everything and everyone. She ran a little hospital (a glorified dispensary) which served all the farms around as well. It saved the Africans a long walk to Nairobi, but the queue of patients might take her up to two hours each morning to see to. No patient was charged a fee and they all loved her dearly.

We never locked the house at night – in fact we had no keys – but we seldom lost anything of value. The house leaked like a sieve, and friends who came to stay were told to bring gumboots in place of bedroom slippers. I would help my mother push the bed round the room as she said: 'Well, dear, we'll give her a nice dry corner for her head and a mackintosh for her feet.'

About this time came the slump. Coffee was selling at 2p a pound. Then the locusts struck: vast swarms that looked like rain from a distance, till you heard the rumble that was the whirring of their wings. Everyone would turn out and stand in their shambas beating *debes* and shouting to try and drive them off. But on they came and settled on everything. In front was green and behind them a desert. I have seen them eat the washing on the line – eat the doormat and the dogs' bed lying in the sun. If you were unlucky enough to be on the road the radiator jammed up till it boiled.

Between bouts of Wispers Olga would dash back to wherever my father was stationed and do her duty as a Provincial Commissioner's wife. Olga's forthright manner, outspokenness and contempt for Government red tape must have caused my father many an embarrassing moment. Once she arrived at Government House with a camp bed under her arm and said she didn't mind how long she waited but she wanted to see HE. She did, about half an hour later.

Oscar came out in 1904 as an Assistant District Commissioner, after serving in the Boer War. He had graduated from Oxford with a double first and was elected a Fellow of All Souls. His chief interests were history and the classics. He became one of Kenya's best Swahili scholars and was an examiner for many years. He met Olga in 1916, a widow of 23 whose husband had been killed in action in the first three months of the war. She received news of this on their farm at Koru by African drum three weeks before the official telegram reached her. She left the farm and became a VAD in Nairobi. Oscar became Chief Native Commissioner with a seat in the Legislative Council. In 1941 Olga was elected to Legco as member for Kiambu, with an overwhelming majority. Oscar was then a member in his official capacity, and she was told that they could not have husband and wife sitting on opposite benches. But she remained in Legco until her sudden death in December 1947. Oscar had died in December 1943. Wispers then passed to us and we uprooted the coffee trees in 1948 – just two years before the boom.

Karen in the Twenties

by F H Sprott

I arrived in Kenya in October 1919. My father, Sir Frederick Sprott, had bought a small property, now known as Cooper's Hill, from Major C Steele. I started to clear the heavy forest and build a couple of cottages for my parents. My father became an Elected Member of Legislative Council.

The Ngong district then stretched from the Maasai boundary to the Dagoretti Forest Reserve, and included the Karen Estate which belonged to a Danish syndicate. Baron and Baroness von Blixen were shareholders. The Baron, a well-known white hunter, was mostly away on safari, and Baroness Karen von Blixen (Isak Dinesen) managed the estate which she subsequently made famous in her book, *Out of Africa*. The property comprised about 4000 acres on the south side of the Nairobi-Ngong road, and about 1000 acres on the north side, where the manager lived in the original Blixen home, which now forms the dining-room of the Westwood Park Country Club.

There was a large acreage of coffee, but much of it was planted on unsuitable land and produced poor returns. In the 1931 slump the company got into difficulties and the land passed into the hands of Mr J R Martin. Later it became the Karen Estate and was developed as a residential property. Karen Blixen's home went to Colonel and Mrs Lloyd and then to their daughter. Finally it was bought by the Danish Government, equipped as a Domestic Science college, and presented to the Government of Kenya as an Uhuru gift.

Another block of land was owned by W McNaughton, always called 'Wully'. The present Warai Roads are not derived from some Maasai word, but from the local pronunciation of Bwana Wully. The present Karen shopping centre was represented by two meat dukas, both owned by Somalis – one by the present occupier, Ali Hassan, the other by Farah Aden. The district abounded in wild animals of all kinds. Leopards and hyenas were plentiful, and at different times we had lion, rhino and buffalo in what is now Muritu Estate, just at the back of us.

Karen Estates

from a brochure published in August 1936

Karen Estates are situated eight miles west of Nairobi, at the foot of the Ngong Hills and at a mean altitude of 6100 feet. Those who think that Kenya is one of the very remote portions of the earth should learn that it is possible to leave Ngong on Monday by Imperial Airways and arrive in London on the following Saturday, and that the 1937 programme of that progressive company aims at halving the duration of this journey. Ngong, an administrative centre of the Maasai Reserve, is a small township situated 14 miles from Nairobi. As to how purely 'African' the district is, as recently as March 1936 baboons inhabited the forests of the Estate, zebra and eland did considerable damage to the golf course, and lion have been known to cause suspension of work among Africans engaged in mowing the greens.

The price of plots, of either ten or twenty acres, ranges from £15 to £32 an acre. The prospective builder can estimate the all-in cost of a stone house with a tiled roof at 9/- per square foot of floor space, or 9d. per cubic foot, which is very much cheaper than in England.

An 18-hole golf course of about 6600 yards is in course of construction. Practically all golf courses in Kenya have what are known as 'browns' instead of greens. These 'browns' are made of murram, and their surface can best be likened to that of an *en-tout-cas* tennis court. The Karen course provides excellent grass greens which are watered daily. Nor is golf here the expensive pastime that it is in England. The local caddie, second to none in his keenness of eyesight, is more than content with a payment, including tip, of 6d. per round.

The first St Francis Church, Karen

'When we went to live in Karen in 1938,' writes Mrs E M Low, 'there was nowhere that we and our neighbours could meet for worship, so my husband built a small thatched church in our garden. When the building was finished the squirrels took possession, so we called it the Church of St Francis.'

The McQueens

by Madge McQueen (Mrs Finlay McNaughton)

James McQueen and his wife, Mary, arrived in Mombasa in 1896 from Dumfries in Scotland, where James had been a blacksmith. They hired a few porters and two donkeys and set forth along the old caravan route to find their future home in the Highlands of Kenya. The theft of a set of razors so angered James that he swore never to shave again, and thereafter was distinguished by his waist-long beard. At one point Mary McQueen actually carried her husband after he had sprained his ankle. She cooked all the meals on a piece of flat iron laid across three stones. Eventually James and Mary were alone on the trail with two donkeys, the porters having deserted. Thus they came to Nairobi.

The McQueens' first camp was at Pangani (near the Forest Road Cemetery); later they camped where the present Museum is sited, near Ainsworth causeway.

From there they moved to Fort Smith, where their eldest son was born in 1897; the eldest daughter, Jean, was born in 1899.

Mary and James then trekked to Uganda and stayed at Busoga, where the second son, James, was born. But Uganda was troubled by mutinies, mosquitoes and famine, and the Warrior King of Bunyoro was threatening to get rid of all white men.

So the McQueens once more moved their goods and chattels, returned to Kenya, and bought the land now known as 'Rhino Park', where they made their permanent home. Madge was born here in 1905, followed by her sisters Minnie (now Mrs McKenzie) and Mary (now Mrs White). James built the house himself, forging his nails just as the Maasai forged their spears. He cleared and planted land on the edge of the Mbagathi River and the family were self-supporting for almost all their needs. Game abounded, rhinos drinking in the stream, elephants trampling the crops and baboons being an everlasting nuisance, besides the herds of zebra and antelopes.

The children grew up in this lovely spot fearless and happy. Mary McQueen made everything they wore, at first from dreadful striped material, then from the khaki cloth that took its place. Shoes were not worn at all by the younger children. Mary taught her children until they were old enough to board at school in Nairobi. Of course all the children spoke and understood Kikuyu and were well versed in Kikuyu customs.

James McQueen the younger and his family continued to live at Rhino Park until 1967, when they sold the residue of the land and moved to another part of the district.

Madge married Finlay McNaughton and they still live on part of the land which belonged to William ('Wully'), Finlay's father, most of which was bought by Karen Estates.

Wilson Airways

In 1929 Mrs Florence Kerr Wilson, 50 years old and recently widowed, flew to England from an airstrip at Langata in a Fokker Universal with Mr Tom Campbell Black as pilot and Mr Archie Watkins as engineer. In those days there were few airstrips, let alone airfields, and no sophisticated instruments. Refuelling arrangements were extremely sketchy. Pilots relied on simple navigation by compass and map and often came down on roads or in the bush. The African services of Imperial Airways had not yet begun.

Tom Campbell Black's ambition was to start a local air transport business, and in Mrs Wilson he found an enthusiastic backer. Wilson Airways was launched on 31 July 1929 with a capital of £50 000 and one Gipsy Moth aircraft. Campbell Black made history by flying a $17\frac{1}{2}$-stone passenger with his baggage to Croydon, England, in this tiny machine, within one week. He flew back in an Avro Five which, with the Gipsy Moth, founded Wilson Airways' fleet. In the first full year's operation the company flew more than 150 000 miles at a cost to passengers of

Top: the Acting Governor, Mr Denham, climbing into a Royal Air Force machine at Nairobi in 1927

Bottom: Mrs Florence Wilson; she and her husband used to farm at Timau before his death in 1928

1/3d. a mile. By 1931 the company had three pilots and a fleet of two Avro Fives, two D H Puss Moths and three Gipsy Moths.

Campbell Black made the first non-stop flight from Zanzibar to Nairobi, and was the first to fly from Nairobi to Mombasa and back in a day. Mrs Wilson piloted herself on occasions, and with Captain C P Mostert flew 8531 miles from Zanzibar to Croydon, via the Congo, Kano and Dakar, in a Puss Moth, in 80 hours and 40 minutes flying time, averaging 106 miles an hour.

At the outbreak of the Second World War pilots and engineers joined the Kenya Auxiliary Air Unit, and later the RAF, and the company ceased to function as an independent airline. It was later merged into East African Airways. Mrs Wilson died in 1966, but the airport at Langata survives. A plaque at Wilson Airport, formerly Nairobi West, commemorates its founder's outstanding services to aviation in Africa.

TWO

LIMURU

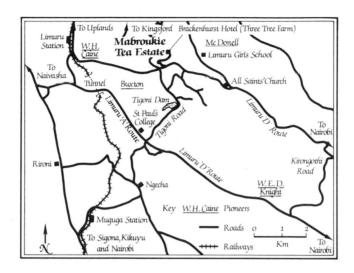

Three Tree Farm

by Margot Howard (formerly Cane)

The arrival of the Uganda Railway at Limuru Station on Christmas Day 1899 was probably the first western impact on a mist-ridden, high-altitude country (around 7200 feet) called Limuru, or by the Africans, Rongai.

Sir Thomas Fowell Victor Buxton was one of the earliest English settlers to arrive, in 1902. His land bordered the railway line and consisted of the usual square mile surveyed by Government and sold to intending settlers. He brought Waswahili up from the coast to grow English potatoes in the rich forest land. Sir Victor gave land to be used for a Deacons' school – now the thriving St Paul's United Theological College. His son, Clarence, developed the land as a dairy and tea estate. Mr Devshanathoo tells me that there were 14 dukas opposite the Post Office in 1914. (He himself is still in Limuru.) Asians started building their dukas on land owned by W H Caine and when, in 1922, the settlers banded together against the Asians, he turned them off. The Asians moved on to township land and Mr Caine lost his only paying crop.

We bought Three Tree Farm from a Mr and Mrs Major in 1914. Mr Major met us at the station with a buggy drawn by two horses. It was dark and misty, and he had enjoyed a long wait in Holmes' store, which possessed a bar. He threw us into the buggy and scrambled into the driver's seat and off we went. One of the horses had been attacked by a lion, had huge claw marks on its back and was terrified by the dark – so were we. It is justifiable to say that there were no roads; only tracks of red mud which became worse during the rains. And how it rained!

My mother, who was an Australian, soon cleaned up the little house, removed monkey cages from the verandah, and proceeded to plant maize and vegetables while my father, after war broke out, became a censor in Nairobi.

Digging land always meant jiggers. Every night when I went to bed the house-servant, Marilu, used to be called in, given a safety-pin and by the light of the hurricane lamp proceed to dig them out of my toes. They had companions called jigger fleas which used to bite into our legs and had to be pulled off. Paraffin was the antidote for all evils and my legs and feet, and indeed my inside (a teaspoonful taken in milk) was always smelling of paraffin. The labour came early, singing,

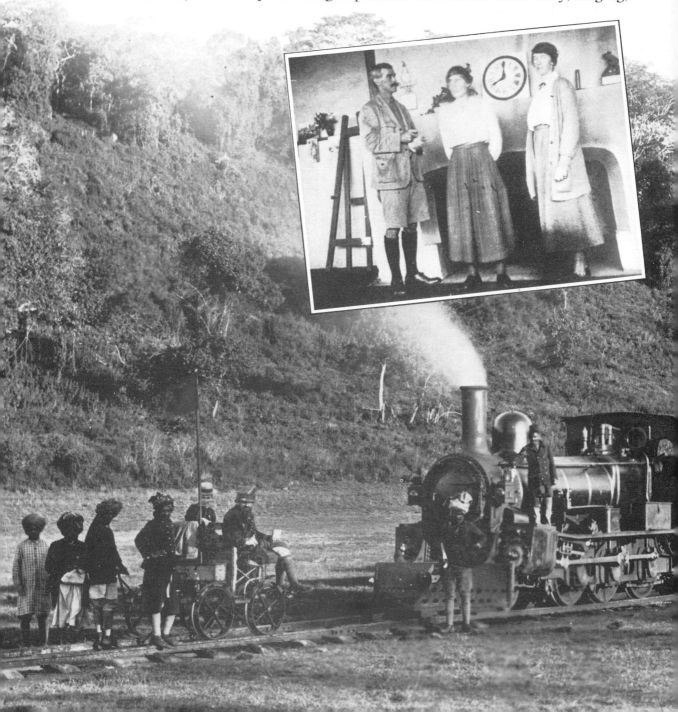

and worked late; mostly they wore soft leather *shukas* dyed in red ochre, and often wore tins filled with snuff, in their ears. They were full of natural politeness and fun.

Since it was wartime we had to live as simply as possible – a sack of *posho*, a sack of sugar, a *debe* of lard from Uplands and those endless Cape Gooseberries. We had an invaluable *fundi*, first an Asian until he was killed in a fight, then an African. Nearly all our furniture was built from petrol boxes.

The owner of the next door farm, Mrs Hirtzel, asked if she could come and live at Three Tree Farm as she hated being alone. My mother was delighted, and the *fundi* built the first round cottage at Brackenhurst. The two women then decided to take convalescent officers as non-paying guests. So more cottages were built, until we were quite a large household. I was sent to school in Nairobi; transport was difficult – many is the time I had to bicycle back to school on Monday mornings, collecting an order mark for being late.

In 1918 the Armistice was signed; but still no ships tied up in Kilindini's new harbour to take Europeans from Uganda and Kenya for their long-postponed visit to Britain.

Top: A B McDonnell founded Limuru Girls' School in 1923;
Mary Roseveare (middle) and Margaret Lister (right) ran it
together

Bottom: Limuru Station

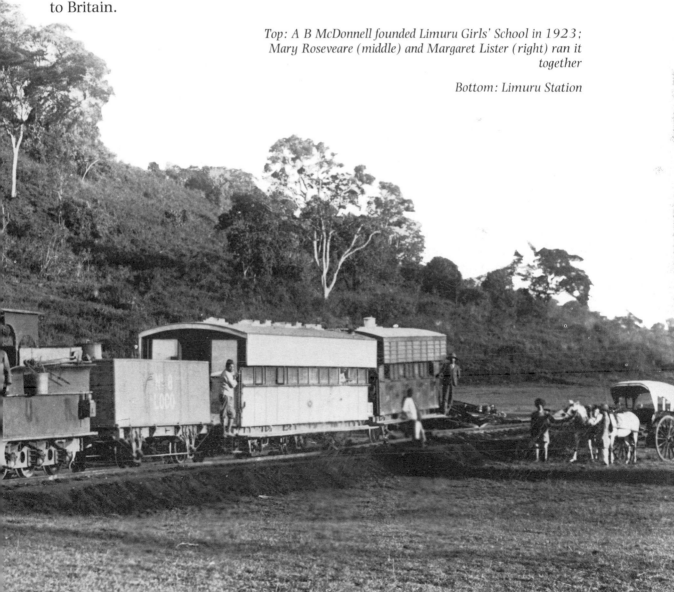

One day a telegram came, carried in a cleft stick, asking my mother if she could accommodate two missionary families from Uganda until their ship arrived. She agreed, and they paid the sum of 7/- each daily, all found – and were the forerunners of Brackenhurst Hotel. For many years Uganda missionaries spent their annual holiday at Brackenhurst on these terms. Later, Government officials and business people came to recuperate from malaria and other tropical illnesses that are now so well contained. The hotel, run by the family, prospered until the 1930 slump. A car used to go to Nairobi on Tuesdays and Fridays taking guests, and enormous bunches of violets, carnations and vegetables to Mr Sands' market. Supplies bought in Nairobi were tied on all round the running boards of the car – 300 eggs fell off one day – and a *toto* used to cling on somewhere behind and report if anything fell off. Another day it was the bag of rupees brought to pay the wages.

Brackenhurst continued in being as a hotel until the 1960s, when it was acquired by the Baptist Church. It is now known as the Baptist Assembly and is used for church gatherings.

Paradise Flycatchers

by C Kingsford

It was in July when a pair of Paradise Flycatchers started to build in the Prunus Priddum – flowering cherry – just outside my bedroom window.

The cock was in splendid plumage with his long chestnut tail, blue-black head, and china-blue rings round his eyes. The nest was sited on a very thin branch, not concealed in any way. Both birds worked at the nest for some three weeks until they had built a lovely little cup of moss and lichen. It was impossible to see into the nest, so I never knew whether one or two eggs were laid – two to three is usual. The cock bird appeared to take longer spells on the nest than the hen. We rather thought that she preferred to do the night shift. Incubation took about three weeks and then a single fledgling was hatched.

At about ten days old the tiny bit of brown fluff sat on the edge of the nest very shakily, and landed on the ground beneath the tree. The parent birds were obviously worried, but nothing like as fussed as a Bulbul who came down beside it and loudly implored the parents, or somebody, to do something about it. I caught the cat and shut him up, then returned the tiny bird to the nest. It was soon down again, and the parents busied themselves supplying it with food while it perched precariously on a flower stem a foot or two above the ground. It was astonishing how soon the little bird became airborne. The family remained in the garden for a few days and then left us.

Last year three Paradise Flycatchers' nests were built in the garden. The first and second met with tragedy. Those vicious predators, the Crowned Hornbills, one day destroyed the first nest and devoured the young. The second had, as usual, been constructed on the flimsiest of twigs, but too insecurely, and when the

KITISURU

KAREN

HILL - NAIROBI

LONDIANI

NJORO

KIPKABUS

KISUMU

RAVINE-SABATIA

parents were coming and going from the edge of the nest, it tilted at a perilous angle and soon the pathetic little body was lying dead on the ground. But all went smoothly with the third nest and two fledglings were successfully reared.

Uplands

Uplands Bacon Factory began when an application in 1906 for 248 acres at Uplands was granted to a London company (East African Estates Ltd.) by the Government of Kenya, on the understanding that the company would start a bacon-curing industry. Pigs were imported from the Seychelles and curing began in a small way in temporary buildings. It was thought at the time that refrigeration was not necessary at such high altitudes – a complete myth, of course.

One for the road

Limuru Sports Club, founded about 1912, was at Limuru Station on the edge of the swamp. It was purely a tennis club. After a hard afternoon's tennis many of the players would move across to the Station Stores for a convivial evening. One member used to bring his servant and a wheelbarrow to ensure his safe return home.

Cash crop

Tea was first planted in Limuru by Mr W H Caine, who obtained his seed from the Director of the Calcutta Botanical Gardens in 1903. A hand-made and sun-dried sample was sent to London for comment in 1909. The report was generous and ended with a valuation of 7d. per pound.

A Farm Manager

by Sir John Hewett

In June 1914, at the age of 19 years, I came to British East Africa as a pupil on the farm of W E D Knight, always known as Wednesday Knight.

I shared a grass hut in the garden with another pupil and was woken at 5 a.m. by Wed and led to the dairy by an African, to supervise the milking. The cows were milked into a variety of old tins, four-gallon paraffin *debes* taking pride of place. I understood not one word of the language and the milkers thought this a great joke, drinking most of the milk and getting me a ticking-off from Wed when we got back to the house.

After breakfast I was given a carriage whip and a scrap of paper inscribed *kazi pesi* and sent to a shamba where 50 Africans were preparing to plant coffee. Nobody was working very hard. The crack of the whip and shouts of *kazi pesi* sent them into ecstasies of mirth. This more or less stopped them from working at all, and encouraged the women and children from a nearby shamba to lay down their *pangas* and join the fun.

After a while we pupils learned the 'language' – a mixture of Swahili, Kikuyu and English. With the help of 250 Africans and a hillside plough we cut what was Chapore Lane and is now Kirongothi Road. The Knights' farm was then about 2400 acres.

One evening Wed arrived back from Nairobi with the news that we were at war. The whole family was in tears, whereas Frank and I could not wait to saddle the ponies and join the East African Mounted Rifles which was forming at the Norfolk Hotel in Nairobi.

In 1916, owing to illness, I returned to Limuru where I was put to 'manage' the Hendersons' farm. 'Manage' is in inverted commas as I really knew nothing about it. The Hendersons owned a lovely farm near the church. The Canes lived at Three Tree Hill, later Brackenhurst. I remember one day riding up to Three Tree Hill (named after three huge *muna* trees which guided wagons trekking from Nairobi) and hearing a series of detonations. I saw a European lady fiddling with something on the ground, then putting up an umbrella and running like a hare. Before she had gone more than a few yards four detonators went off in quick succession and rocks flew in all directions. This was Mrs Cane blasting rock to make the road and saving on fuse wire, which was very difficult to come by.

Various modes of transport were used. Mrs McDonell had a nice bath-chair pulled by three Africans. Commander and Mrs Nivison had a dog-cart. But mostly people walked or rode ponies, donkeys or mules, and transported their babies in hammocks slung on a bamboo pole and carried by two Africans.

On one occasion the first Mrs Leakey, Canon Leakey's wife, took a rickshaw from the Stanley Hotel. All the way the rickshaw men chanted their songs of the fat old cow they were pushing up-hill. On arrival they held out their hands for baksheesh. Alas, Mrs Leakey understood Kikuyu. In her turn she chanted: 'The fat old cow is dry.'

Mrs Hudson Cane and staff, building the road to Brackenhurst in 1915

THREE
KIAMBU AND RUIRU

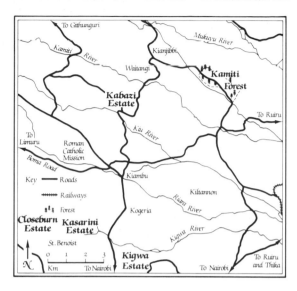

The District and its Coffee

Kiambu township is ten miles, Ruiru about 15, from the centre of Nairobi. Kiambu is an area with a great variety of natural beauty on the lower slopes of the Aberdares. Many streams flowing south-east from the Kinangop (12 816 feet) and its foothills to join the Athi River cut the district into a series of steep ridges and valleys.

In the higher country, up to 8000 feet, bracken grows and the clear streams that emerge from the forest tumble over sizeable waterfalls. Once the whole of this higher country was forest, but only a few patches remain. It is now all a mosaic of shambas, closely and industriously cultivated, with many small houses. Here and there are plantations of eucalyptus or macrocarpa, and gardens of recently planted tea. Lower down, the main cash crop is coffee, often shaded with grevillea trees.

Most of the big coffee plantations are on the south-eastern borders of the district, between 6000 and 5000 feet, where the ridges slope down towards the Athi Plains.

At the end of the nineteenth century a great famine, plus outbreaks of smallpox, and of rinderpest among the cattle, drove the Kikuyu people back across the Chania River towards the Kinangop and their original home near Fort Hall (Murang'a). So when the Europeans arrived most of the land was uncultivated, covered with thick bush and scrub, and 'empty' of people. Wild animals were there in profusion – almost every species now to be seen in game parks lived freely and roamed the countryside.

The history of coffee-planting starts about 1902 when all the land near Nairobi was opened for development by European settlers, and leased by the Government in lots of 640 acres. In Kiambu, settlement began along the Nairobi-Kiambu road and also from the old Fort Hall road, along the banks of the Kamiti. First the forest, and bush six to eight feet high, had to be cleared by hand; once it was cleared, it was impossible to know what to plant. Labourers, like their masters, were inexperienced, roads non-existent, houses primitive and malaria rife.

Wheat, barley, maize, tobacco, citrus and other fruit trees, and nearly all the English vegetables were planted with varying success before coffee emerged as the main crop. By 1904 Messrs Felix and Favre, on the farm known as St Benoist and later as Cheleta, had 100 trees bearing their first crop, 9000 plants from six to 12 inches high, and 12 000 seedlings in a coffee nursery. No one else in Kiambu could boast of having bearing coffee in 1904. J R Wood at Kasarini had 500 plants 18 months old, 'looking strong and well', and Lady Delamere on Kigwa River had from 25 000 to 30 000 about six months old in her nursery, and 3400 about 12 months old planted out, 'all looking very healthy'. Lady Delamere did not live on this farm, which was run for her by J R Wood. The Roman Catholic Mission on Riara River was said to be irrigating 400 trees, age unknown.

Development from the old Fort Hall road (now the Kamiti road) began with J S Hall and T Russell, both at Kamiti by 1904, and rapidly spread upwards to the borders of the Kikuyu Reserve.

The Findlay family, so well-known in Kiambu, deserve a special mention. Mr Kenneth Findlay arrived at Waitangi in 1913. There were four sons, three of whom took over parts of the family estates after their father's death and lived in Kiambu all their lives. All the brothers served in the First World War; the eldest lost his life in the Dardanelles, while the other three were all awarded the Military Cross.

Bottom left: in 1912 Major Symes-Thompson of Kianjibbi Estate was woken at dawn to be told that lions had killed some of his trek oxen in the night. He summoned two neighbours and the farm labour and they killed these six animals before breakfast.

Right: Kiltannon

Houses

The first houses consisted of round grass or mud huts, and when more rooms were needed another hut was added. A separate kitchen made of corrugated iron, and often boasting the only chimney in the house, stood apart from the other huts.

However, there were some more ambitious houses even as early as 1904. Lady Delamere imported a house for her manager. It was in sections, composed of wood and corrugated iron, with patterned ceilings of pressed steel, and pinewood floors. The original house at what is now Kiltannon comprised a verandah and five rooms. The pressed steel ceilings were found to be too hot and were replaced with wooden ones, but two survive – one patterned with elegant sprays of flowers, the other like a block of chocolate.

The house on Kogeria was also built in 1904, by John Ellis, who came from India. This has immensely high rooms. The walls are actually 17 feet high, topped with pressed steel ceilings as at Kiltannon, but because of the height these were not found to be too hot and all have been preserved. Kogeria was built locally by Indian *fundis* and had the first built-in kitchen in the district, probably the first in Kenya. The second owner removed it to a suitable distance away from the house as was the custom at that time.

The usual type of farm house, after the grass hut stage, was of wood and iron. Perhaps the largest was Philip Coldham's, built in 1912 and still standing. It measures 5000 square feet (100 × 50 feet), which was very large for those days, and only cost £600 to build. Archdeacon Low called it 'a railway station in a wilderness'.

A day's shopping from Ruiru

This wasn't easy. A pony and two-wheeled cart with one seat was the usual means of transport. The seat was hinged and a small box-like compartment under it held a few small parcels. The driver had to balance on the seat while the cart lurched from side to side into potholes. If the pothole was unduly large, he took a header over the wheel. The pony was well trained to stand still while his driver recovered. On arrival in Nairobi he was put up at Murrell's stable on the corner of Ronald Ngala Street and Moi Avenue, where there was piped water.

After a lunch at the Carlton Grill in Government Road (Moi Avenue now), where excellent steaks or mutton chops were grilled on an open fire, the traveller started the return journey about 3.30 p.m. and reached his farm soon after 6 p.m. During the rains, three or four weeks would elapse before another journey could be undertaken.

After 1912 we were able to go to Nairobi on the famous Thika Tramway. Trains stopped at J R Wood's siding. While Mrs Wood set off to the siding in a pony-trap in good time for the train, her husband was often late and would have to run for it in his slippers, his servant hurrying after him with his shoes. Another unpunctual passenger, this time for the return journey, was Mrs Lizzie Barnes who, with her brother Bob Udall, ran the Ruiru General Stores, and later the Red Lion. The train would wait at Nairobi Station until Lizzie had finished her shopping and was ready to return to Ruiru.

Mr Ake Bursell and helper hull-down at Kalimoni in 1919. Mr Bursell was the first farmer in Ruiru to grow sisal on black cotton soil. He built the factory for the Bag and Cordage Company which was started in 1937

An unlucky lion

by Margit Bursell

My husband went to East Africa in 1913 to start coffee on Baroness Blixen's farm at Ngong. Later he returned to Europe and started a company in Sweden to grow sisal. In 1918 he bought 1000 acres below Ruiru, cleared part of it and planted the sisal and imported machinery to turn the leaves into fibre. We also had about 90 acres of coffee, a dairy herd and breeding pigs, so farm life had really started.

All this time we lived on game which we shot on Sundays. One Sunday I had been lucky with the gun the whole morning, and driving home I saw a warthog with his wife and children staring at us. I had never tasted wild pork so thought I would have a shot at him, missed, and saw the whole family happily trotting off. I thought no more about it until after tea when an African came to the door and asked why we did not come out to collect our lion. We saddled up and rode to where the African directed us and there was a beautiful lion lying with his head in his paws. He must have been lying up in the bush when I missed my warthog, and just managed to walk down the donga. I don't think many people can boast of having shot a lion without setting eyes on it.

Sir Northrup McMillan

by John Carver

William Northrup McMillan, a very rich American sportsman, later knighted for his war-time services to Britain, acquired land some 20 miles from Nairobi in the early 1900s. At that time no one man was allowed to lease more than 5000 acres on a 99 year lease at an annual rent of $\frac{1}{2}$d. per acre. In the early maps the area known as 'Juja' was divided into blocks marked 'Mr McMillan's land', 'Major Ringer's land', 'Major Bulpitt's land', etc., Mr McMillan having used the names of his friends to acquire 19 000 acres. Later on he added more acres to Juja on the Nairobi side of the Ruera River, and then bought Donyo Sabuk estate comprising 6900 acres.

The estate was called after two West African images brought to Kenya by Northrup McMillan and known as Ju and Ja. Numerous superstitions surrounded them, and eventually Lady McMillan buried them somewhere in the Ndarugu Valley, but she never disclosed where. One of the superstitions was that the images would bring bad luck to the idols' owners, some of whom would die at sea. Sir Northrup McMillan died at sea off Mombasa on a return journey from England.

In 1905 the pre-fabricated sections of Juja House arrived from England, ending their journey by mule-cart from Nairobi. Juja was soon a thriving community with an area of one square mile enclosed in a ten-foot fence on three sides, with the river as the fourth protection to keep out wild animals. Within the compound was a post office and a telegraph office, and housing for a European staff consisting of a manager, a chauffeur, two gardeners, a groom, a storeman and Lady McMillan's maid. There was stabling for 26 horses, which were carefully netted in at night against the dreaded tsetse fly. Each horse had its own syce who slept and ate with it and ran alongside when it was ridden out, ready to take the reins at any time.

There were also caged wild animals, including a lion, which were chained by day to iron rings set in concrete just outside the front door at Juja House. Billiam Webb, a neighbour, was invited to lunch one day and bicycled the odd 15 miles down the dusty, hot road to find that a lioness was on heat and a wild male lion in attendance. Sir Northrup was seated on the verandah chuckling with delight, whilst his guests and servants had sought refuge in a loft. Billiam was bidden to

Mr L D Galton Fenzi of Kigwa Estate founded the Automobile Association in Nairobi. He and Captain Gethin made the first journey by car from Nairobi to Mombasa in 1926

enter, but he leapt on his bicycle and headed for home, minus his drink and lunch.

Juja House was surrounded by formal gardens and approached by an avenue of trees, plants and flowers. Below the house were large fruit and vegetable gardens, also grain and maize. Attempts were made to farm ostriches, pigs, cattle and sheep, but all were more or less defeated by disease. However, a slaughterhouse, bacon factory, dairy and cheese factory were built, also an elaborate block of stone pig houses. From this ran a light railway to facilitate cleaning out the pig houses. Juja was famed for its hospitality and there was a camping site set aside for any passing safaris. Colonel Theodore Roosevelt was on one of these safaris, and stayed at Juja for some time.

During his stay he and Sir Northrup had a party in Nairobi. Afterwards, feeling that the night was yet young, they took two stone idols from the gate of the Khoja Mosque. These were placed by the fireplace in the McMillan's Nairobi house, Chiromo. A few days later, when the hue and cry was at its height, the District Commissioner called on other business and saw the images. In order to avoid a scandal (particularly as Colonel Roosevelt was shortly to stand for election in America) the DC advised Sir Northrup to dispose of the idols as quickly and quietly as possible. Nothing more was heard of them until about 1937, when some thorn trees were being removed on Juja and the idols came to light. At first they were thought to be the missing Ju and Ja, but were later identified by the British Museum and exhibited.

From 1914 to 1918 Juja House was a hospital and convalescent home for British officers. Having attempted all kinds of farming without success, Sir Northrup sold the estate in 1919 to Mr F N Nettlefold, a wealthy Englishman, and went to live at Donyo Sabuk House, which he had recently built. He became enormous, weighing, it was said, over 20 stone. When sitting in an ordinary motor car, one leg and almost half the rest of him overflowed. The National Bank of India had a seat made specially to hold him.

He was buried on Ol Donyo Sabuk. The hearse was made with skis on the bottom and a tractor pulled it up the hill, followed by the mourners. Many cars burned out their clutch-plates, and when the tractor eventually reached the shoulder of the hill it also stopped, so the burial took place there instead of at the top, which had been the original plan. Oak trees were planted by the grave.

The Bombax

The pink-flowered bombax, a cousin of the kapok said to be native to Ceylon, is among our more beautiful exotic flowering trees. Its wood is used largely for tea chests. For many years the only bombax in Kenya was in Miss Olive Collyer's garden at Kabete, grown from seed from Madeira; she could never propagate it and it never formed seed. In 1939 Major H F Ward of Kabazi Estate brought in more seed from Madeira which he gave to the Forest Department, saying they could give him half of what came up. Boxfuls germinated, and Major Ward had more plants than he could do with. Kabazi has a large area covered with them – a wonderful sight just before the long rains, which is when they flower. These trees are also common in and around Nairobi, having been planted from the remainder of Major Ward's original seedlings.

Captain Tony Gladstone, AFC

by J K Twist

On 28 November 1924 Captain Tony Gladstone, AFC, set out from London with Captain T K Twist on a safari from Cairo to Kisumu, arriving in March 1925. They followed the Nile, as far as it was possible to do so, with the object of surveying and planning a route for a flying boat service from Khartoum to Lake Victoria. The proposal was to carry air mail to Cairo from East Africa and the Sudan, and gold from the Congo, and eventually to extend the service to the Cape. After taking part in this expedition Captain Twist bought a coffee farm in Kiambu and settled there.

They had an eventful journey, partly by river steamer and partly by bicycle. From Rejaf to Nimule (100 miles) they rode second-hand bicycles bought in Khartoum; these were always breaking down and were eventually abandoned, and they reached Nimule on foot. They received no encouragement for their scheme at first; in fact Sir Geoffrey Archer, Governor of the Sudan, told them to pack their kit and return to England. But in Kenya Lord Delamere gave strong support to the scheme, as did Kenneth Archer and the Chamber of Commerce. As a result, in October 1925 £2000 was voted by the Kenya Legislative Council to test the possibilities of air communication between Khartoum and Kisumu.

In November 1926 Captain Gladstone brought out a sea-plane with a Jupiter engine, which he named the 'Pelican'. Unfortunately it was so badly damaged by hitting a submerged object in the Nile at Khartoum that it had to be written off. The British Air Ministry then lent him a Fairey sea-plane in which he made several flights between Kisumu and Khartoum. But again there was a stroke of bad luck. When taking off at Kisumu in March 1927 the pilot, not Captain Gladstone, crashed, and the sea-plane was another write-off.

By this time Tony Gladstone had proved his scheme's feasibility. Fresh proposals were made in February 1928 by the Blackburn Aeroplane Company and Sir Alan Cobham's Aviation Company to the three East African Governments, and to the Sudan Government. Subsequently the interests of the new Cobham-Blackburn Company were acquired by Imperial Airways. This company started a flying boat service between Cairo and Kisumu. Later on the flying boats were discarded in favour of land planes, and thus began the air services between Europe and East Africa which have grown to what they are today, Imperial Airways having changed to British Airways.

Tony Gladstone was the real pioneer of civil aviation in East Africa. When he arrived in March 1925 there were no aircraft or landing grounds whatsoever. It was a tragedy he was killed in a flying accident in South Africa, together with Lt Cdr Glen Kidston, in May 1931, and so never saw the results of his pioneering efforts.

Captain Gladstone and Captain Twist

FOUR
KIKUYU AND MUGUGA

February 1963; a deaf boy learns to speak with the aid of pictures at Dagoretti Children's Centre. The Centre is on the site of the old Government boma, *close to Lugard's trading fort*

Origins

In 1890 Frederick Lugard, then in the service of the Imperial British East Africa Company, entered into blood-brotherhood with a number of Kikuyu at Dagoretti. He negotiated for a site on which to build a food depôt and trading fort with the famous Waiyaki. Lugard recorded that:

> 'together they selected a charming site a little distance from the cultivation and villages. A clear mountain stream flowed at the foot of the slope, beyond was the dense forest, in the rear was another stream. Timber and fuel were of course in abundance. The name of the place was Dagoretti.'

The foundations of this first stockade can still be traced near Kihumo Church, but it was abandoned in 1891 after renewed clashes with the local people.

Captain Eric Smith built the next fort in this area at Kabete, where cultivation was advancing into dense forest. The local Kikuyu seemed pleased to have a regular market for their produce. But in 1892 Chief Waiyaki was arrested for an alleged assault upon Captain Purkiss, the Commandant of Fort Smith at the time. The Chief was taken to Kibwezi for trial, but died on arrival. Purkiss also died at Kibwezi, in 1894, and was buried beside Chief Waiyaki in the little graveyard there.

Close on the heels of the Company's officers came the first Christian missionaries. On 6 July 1891 a team left London for Mombasa to establish an Industrial Mission at Dagoretti. However, Kikuyuland was in such a turbulent state that Dr Stewart of Lovedale in South Africa, who headed the mission, chose instead a site at Kibwezi, where work was begun.

It was a disastrous choice, being an unhealthy and sparsely populated area between the Kamba and Maasai. By 1894 only Thomas Watson was left out of the original team of seven.

In September of that year, 1894, he went to Kikuyu to see whether the original plan of establishing a mission at Dagoretti could be revived. Before he could do anything he was recalled to Kibwezi following the mysterious disappearance of Dr Charters, who had been left in charge. Dr Charters had gone out on a shooting expedition with a bearer, and never returned. No trace of them was ever discovered, so it was assumed that they had fallen in with a band of Maasai and been murdered. It was not until October 1897 that Watson was authorized to transfer the mission, and work began on the Dagoretti site on 17 April 1898. The transfer was complete by 11 September 1898. As Thomas Watson was leaving Kibwezi on 27 August, the first railway engine reached the station an hour before his departure.

The Kikuyu Mission

In early 1899 the Kikuyu people were in a sorry plight. The rains had failed for three successive years, famine conditions prevailed and smallpox had broken out. Thomas Watson and his bride, who had just arrived from England, set up a famine relief camp and treated the smallpox victims as best they could. Mrs Watson wrote:

> 'Just what even the little we could do meant, will be better realized
> when I tell you that no Kikuyu would go near a smallpox patient or
> help to bury the dead.'

Another missionary referred to those streams which were still flowing as being choked with corpses.

When the situation improved, Watson organized brick-making beside the Nyongara River, on what is now Alliance High School land. Some of those bricks used in the early buildings are built into the north gable above the main entrance to the Church of the Torch. This church was built between 1928 and 1933 to

This house, the first to be put up at Kikuyu for the Church of Scotland missionaries, was erected by railway engineers in about 1902

replace an open-air church in the forest, whose pews were rough tree trunks supported on stumps, capable of seating 2500 worshippers.

Medical work began under Dr Homer. One of his first actions was to secure the removal in 1912 of the mission to the high ridge where it stands at present, and which at that time was under original forest – cedar, podocarpus, camphor, olive and some hardwoods. The first dispensary was a circular hut sited on the ridge overlooking the Nyongara River. John Paterson, an agricultural missionary, ran a flourishing shamba on the lower site where he grew and distributed the first coffee seedlings, from seeds brought to Kibwezi from Sheikh Othman (a Church of Scotland mission near Aden).

On 4 December 1900 Thomas Watson died of pneumonia. Mrs Watson, widowed after one short year of married life, carried on alone, continuing relief work, building up her tiny school, and providing evening classes for about 40 workmen. She remained a much-beloved member of the mission until her retirement in May 1931, and was affectionately known to her large mission family and beyond as Grannie Watson.

In 1900 the general management of the mission was taken over by the Church of Scotland, with a handsome endowment of £50 000 from the IBEA Company. The Church of Scotland's first ordained missionary, Clement Scott, arrived from Nyasaland in 1901. He was the visionary among the early leaders, seeing Kikuyu as a great educational centre for East Africa, the sheet anchor of a chain of mission stations 'stretching from Lake Victoria to the Horn of Africa and stemming the onslaught of Islam from the north'. He secured for the mission the grant of a large estate, 3000 acres. Shortly before his death in 1907 he baptized the first convert. He and his wife Edith are buried in the graveyard at Kikuyu.

His replacement, Henry Scott – no relation of Clement's – who arrived in January 1908, was a remarkably versatile man – a doctor of medicine and a minister of religion, with the vision to see what was needed and the drive to get it done. Under his leadership the Kikuyu Mission developed apace, and new missions were opened at Tumutumu, near Nyeri, and among the Meru at Chogoria. Scott cycled to Nairobi every Sunday afternoon to take a church service for English-speaking people, and on moonlight nights cycled home again the same evening. This developed into the St Andrew's congregation, Nairobi. When he wrote his last report in 1911 the church numbered 23 communicants and 42 catechumens. School attendance averaged 100 and the teachers' training class had risen to 22. There were three out-station schools, a night school for young men, and dormitories for both boys and girls. The first industrial apprentices had been indentured and the training of hospital assistants begun.

Henry Scott died of dysentery complicated by malaria on 11 April 1911 and was buried at Kikuyu. He was succeeded in the following year by Dr J W Arthur, who had come to Kikuyu in 1907: a man of great personal charm and driving force, who exercised a tremendous influence over the younger Kikuyu. His habit of wearing a rosebud or carnation in his lapel is perpetuated by some of the leading politicians of the present day who were small children at Kikuyu in the late twenties.

The Mission and the First President

Mzee Jomo Kenyatta, first President of Kenya, came to the mission school at the age of about ten, to be enrolled as its 35th pupil. Here at Kikuyu he received his basic education in English, arithmetic, Bible study and carpentry training. He helped Mr Arthur Ruffell Barlow with the first translation of the New Testament into the Kikuyu language. In 1907 Dr Arthur operated on his leg, probably saving his life. In August 1914 he was baptized Johnstone Kamau, and in 1919 married Grace Wahu. They lived at Dagoretti on land given to him by the father of a former Commissioner of Police, Bernard Hinga. Their son, Peter Muigai, and daughter, Margaret Wambui, were brought up at Dagoretti. Margaret Wambui came to the Alliance High School as the thousandth student in 1947. James Muigai, the late President's brother, was the first student to enrol at the Alliance High School when it opened in 1926.

On 17 April 1965 Mzee Kenyatta laid the foundation stone of the Mount Kenya Ward for women and the operating theatre of the mission's Kikuyu Hospital. This had started life in 1908 as the Hunter Memorial with eight beds. Now it treats over 3000 patients (not counting out-patients) each year and has 50 students in training. In 1963 it had its first Kikuyu Matron, Mrs Kimani Nyoike, who was educated at Tumutumu Mission and was the first African State Registered Nurse.

Alliance High School

Under Dr Arthur's leadership the mission forged ahead. The first African boys' boarding school started in 1907. Many parents in those days opposed the school education of their children, especially of their daughters, and had to be persuaded and cajoled. Gradually numbers built up until a secondary school that would take its pupils to college entrance levels could be envisaged.

With the backing of the Government, the Phelps-Stokes Commission in America, British missionary societies, the settlers' leaders – Lord Delamere was a member of the original Board – and generous individuals (a Nairobi business man, Mr Ernest Carr, gave £10 000), the Alliance High School was opened in 1926 with 26 pupils. It was under the management of the Alliance of Protestant Missionary Societies.

Probably no single school has ever exercised more influence over a whole generation than Alliance. A very high proportion of Kenya's future leaders – Cabinet Ministers, civil servants, ambassadors, teachers, business men – were educated here. All honour the name of its great headmaster, Edward Carey Francis: in the words of one Minister, 'the most unforgettable man I ever knew'. At his death, over half the members of the Council of Ministers were old boys of the school. Carey Francis was head of Alliance from 1940 to 1962. He had been a Fellow of Peterhouse and had taught Mathematics at Cambridge. He came to Kenya in 1928 and taught first at Maseno.

Alliance was a pioneer. Today it is one of about a thousand secondary schools in Kenya, but its reputation still stands very high.

Carey Francis

a tribute by Joel Ojal (by courtesy of the East African Standard)

Carey Francis was like a candle that burnt itself out, giving light at its own expense for the benefit of those around him.

I first met Mr Francis in 1928 when I was only a child. He had a strange way of inspiring people. To children he was charming and had many ways of amusing them. His conjuring tricks were always a great attraction.

But that was only one side of Carey. He believed that he could do all things through Christ, the source of his strength.

Carey was a very good footballer and joined the Maseno First Eleven. He was also a good boxer although he never once had to use his skill as a boxer to defend himself. He used Christ as a shield.

Carey was a teacher, an inspector of schools, a mathematician, a geographer, an economist, a linguist and even a musician. When there was no one to play the harmonium he did, although using only his right index finger!

Carey Francis

All Old Boys will remember him as a man with a wonderful memory. On the day of arrival of the new boys, he met them all, and the following day he would call any of them by name. Twenty years later he would still remember them. Their welfare was very much his concern once they had passed through his hands.

All Old Boys will agree that Carey died the way he could have wished to die. He died teaching, at his desk and in the school. His body will lie at the place to which it belongs, the Alliance.

Scouts

Scouting at Alliance, writes James S Smith, began one weekend in April 1927 when a group of seven boys, with their Scoutmaster, held a camp at the source of the Athi River near Ngong.

The boys showed their Scoutmaster how to follow the tracks of a leopard; how to make huts from natural vegetation – they had no tents in those days; how to interpret correctly the sounds of the forest. The Scoutmaster in his turn showed the boys how to make plaster casts of animal tracks; how to improvise grease traps; how to make camping gadgets. They ran out of matches. One of the Scouts showed the Scoutmaster how to make fire by friction, using two pieces of wood, one hard, one soft. Thereafter instead of the Tenderfoot Test which reads: 'lay and light a fire using two matches only,' the Troop's own rule became: 'lay and light a fire using no matches.'

The Alliance High School Troop, which was the first African Scout Troop in Kenya, has had an interesting membership. The names J S Gichuru, E W Mathu, (Dr) Njoroge Mungai, J D Otiende, (Dr) J Kiano, R J Ngala, J J M Nyagah, C Njonjo, R S Matano all appear among the Patrol Leaders at one time or another.

The first pupils of the Alliance Girls' High School, Kikuyu, 1948; Miss Margaret Kenyatta is on the left

Bird paintings by J. M. Belfrage
from the Kiambu and Ruiru Scrapbook.
Left: Scarlet-breasted Sunbird.
Below left: Cinnamon chested Bee-eater.
Below right: Paradise Flycatcher.

In the early days of settlement, the Subukia Valley was renowned for the many species of beautiful butterflies. The large Swallow-tail Papllios, Mackinnionii, Noblis, Phorcas and Bromius were to be seen everywhere; the smaller but no less vivid Precis and Pieridae abounded in the warmer, dryer areas. The elusive and fast-flying Charaxes could be found feeding on their favourite trees, becoming so intoxicated as to allow easy capture.

An evening stroll in the garden, when the sun is setting, will reveal the presence of the many Sphingidea, or Hawk-moths, darting from flower to flower, all busy collecting their evening meal. The large Emperors like the pink and brown Veined Emperor, with its R.A.F. wings and fat pink abdomen, usually hide during the day-light hours, but, attracted to any bright light, will emerge at night. But it is the minute species that are the gems of the Lepidoptera world. Delicate greens, yellows and browns, with spots or stripes in gold and silver, their beauty can only be admired with the aid of a magnifying glass. They pass through life unappreciated and unnoticed.

Two watercolours by H.R.H. Princess Alice, Duchess of Gloucester. Top: Sir Piers Mostyn's house near Naro Moru.
Bottom: a view near Isiolo, Northern Kenya.

Settlers

Possibly the first European settler at Kikuyu was Robert Bladen-Taylor, a journalist and contemporary of Rudyard Kipling, who came from India about 1898 and became a fuel contractor for the railway. He established a homestead at Lengenny Farm and, with his wife, served teas at Kikuyu Station.

The early settlers started by planting coffee. Later they felled the indigenous forest and planted black wattle. Later still they tried flax, pyrethrum, potatoes and many other crops until the district eventually settled down as a dairy farming area.

Wattle

Black wattle was first grown to supply wood fuel to the railway. Later it was grown mainly for the sake of its bark, which contains tannin. A tannin extract factory was built by Mr Berkeley-Matthews in 1929 near Sigona Golf Club. The demand for wattle extract eventually declined as plastics were used more for shoes. Most of the wattle in Kikuyu was cut down in the 1950s, first to build the emergency villages and later for fencing and building when the land was consolidated.

Belvedere Estate

by A Laetitia Nicholas

This farm, only 13 miles from Nairobi, was carved out of the bush in about 1927 by my husband, Wing Commander G B Nicholas DFC, who was killed on active service in 1943 in North Africa. The house consisted of several large rooms on the first floor and nothing below except some rather eerie godowns and vast archways. This was soon converted into a comfortable farmhouse with up-to-date conveniences. The downstairs was filled in, walls and windows put in place, and now it resembles an old hall with its plain stone walls, huge beams and heavy imported furniture.

I wanted some fresh and reliable milk for my three children and so we bought a few cows, all good foundation Friesian stock. A cattle dip then became essential and, as this cost several hundred pounds, it warranted more than just a few house-cows. So we bought some pure-bred Friesians from Major Pirie of Karirana Farm, Limuru. This started off the dairy with some 30 gallons a day. Gradually it grew; more cowstalls, a small milking shed with a three-unit Alfa 10-volt milking machine, then a dairy with a small cooler, etc.

On the outbreak of the Second World War my husband rejoined the RAF and I took over the farm. With the help of a Goan manager, Mr Antonio Pereira, we managed not only to carry on but gradually to expand and improve.

New bull-yards were erected, and calf-pens and a milking parlour for some 80 cows. We installed a larger cold-room, with Hall's thermostatic refrigeration plant. The milking parlour was 80 per cent dust-proof, with neon lighting. The entire herd was tuberculin tested and a ten-unit gasoline milking plant erected.

Production rose, and in 1947 Belvedere Estate, consisting of 250 acres all under Kikuyu grass, produced 100 000 gallons of milk in 365 days. Since then the re-aligned railway has come through the farm, cutting off a considerable portion, and inevitably production has decreased.

Many years have gone by, some happy and some sad. The old house is still the home of the Nicholas family, or of all that are left.

After all these years of striving and working, I look on my lawn and see forest trees which I planted in time gone by. Now they are enormous, and two people holding hands could not encircle the trunks. I go to my dairy and see over 8000 bottles in the sterilizing cabinet ready to be filled by the automatic filler machine. We have nearly 4000 customers to whom bottled milk is delivered daily. The nine three-ton lorries leave the farm at 2 a.m. with their full load. We buy milk from nearby farmers and process it. We sell over 2000 gallons a day.

It is quite an achievement, for which I must again thank my Goan manager, Mr Antonio Pereira, who has been with the farm for 38 years. His children, and mine, were brought up on this farm. The house looks a bit weather-beaten but its Golden Shower and Virginia Creeper seem to cuddle it from foundation to roof. On my upstairs verandah I can overlook most of the farm, all neatly contoured and terraced on the steep slopes, all paddocked in roughly 20-acre paddocks as far as the eye can see, before the farm dips down to the river. My four-acre garden is very colourful with big lawns and herbaceous borders and trim macrocarpa hedges, all of which I planted.

Now in 1967 Belvedere is sold. In a few months I shall leave it and feast my eyes on its glory of colour for the last time, because I shall never return to it. I want its beauty to remain in my memory for the years I still have left in this world.

I am a Kenyan, and wish my successors good luck and prosperity. I shall not leave Kenya because I feel part of it and its people, if they will put up with an old woman who has helped in a small way to develop a tiny corner of the country.

A local enterprise

Mr Popatlal had a useful small industry at Kikuyu Station making hasps, staples, padlocks, bolts and hinges out of scrap metal and old oil drums. He made the machinery for the factory here at Kikuyu himself. His products went all over East Africa during the Second World War, when there were few imports.

FIVE

THIKA

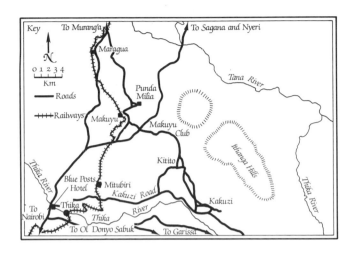

A long walk to Karamaini

by C W P Harries

Early in 1904 Father, my brother Cecil, Uncle Willy and a friend set out on foot to inspect the various areas in which land for settlement was being offered by the Protectorate Government. (It was all in districts supposed not to be occupied by Africans, in so-called 'buffer areas' between peoples often at war). They had to carry all their requirements and had no horses.

The first area they inspected was Limuru, Kiambu, Thika, Makuyu and Ruiru. Having done this they went to the second area, Nyeri, Nanyuki and Timau. They walked all round and up the hills and then decided to inspect the third area, Naivasha. So from Timau they walked over Mount Kinangop and round Lake Naivasha. They caught a train to Lumbwa and walked all round Kericho and Sotik.

They only took bare necessities, and slept on the ground in the open. None of them had raincoats and each time a storm of rain came they were drenched. They all wore huge Indian pith helmets, and Uncle Willy objected to getting wet, so whenever rain started he stripped and put all his clothes under his helmet and marched on, starkers. When the rain stopped he would dress and be quite dry whilst the others were shivering in their wet clothes.

On completing Kericho-Sotik they walked to Port Florence, now called Kisumu, and took the train back to Nairobi. Father decided that he liked the Chania Bridge area best. (The name Thika was adopted later.) He then came out with a Government surveyor and put in one peg, not far from the Ndarugu Heights signboard, and told the surveyor that he wanted four 5000 acre farms, two for himself and two for his son-in-law, Herbert Cowie, Mervyn Cowie's father. The dividing line between his and his son-in-law's farm had to be a straight line from the peg to the Aberdares. Father's two farms were from the left of the straight line, along the Kikuyu land unit, down the Theririka and so back to the peg. Mother, my sister Ina, my brother Oswald and I arrived in Nairobi in July 1904. Mother brought in the first piano and the first real cooking stove to British East Africa. I was four years old and was carried out to our farm, Karamaini, on an African's back, and have been there ever since.

There were thousands of acres of forest then and our farm was full of game. Right through it ran a deep elephant track that had to be filled up before we could plough. Buffalo skeletons were everywhere. The forest was full of very large game pits which were used to trap buffalo, and to this day the remains of these pits can be found. Seventeen rhino were shot on the farm, many lions, and over 50 pythons, one of them 23 feet long. Red-legged Spurfowl were so plentiful that the *totos* used to trap them and sell ten for one rupee. We used to cage the birds, as they proved one of our staple foods.

In 1917 I trapped 37 leopards. I shot the one and only lion in my life at the age of 11. I was given a 20-bore shotgun and used to make my own cartridges, using blasting powder. One day I ran short of pellets and very foolishly used old gramophone needles. I killed a warthog with this queer cartridge but it ruined my gun. I received a good hiding and was forbidden to do any shooting for a year.

My brothers tried rearing ostriches. They marked nests on the Tana plains and herded the chicks back to Karamaini, where they were penned. When the feathers were ready, my brothers took them to Kisii and exchanged them for cattle – the number that could be held between thumb and forefinger bought one cow. Then the cattle were driven down to the Nairobi area to be sold for cash. Feathers were also exported until suddenly the fashion changed and ostrich farming came to an end.

In 1910 Father planted our first coffee trees, really because Mother thought the bush so attractive with its glossy leaves, fragrant white flowers and red berries. By 1955 there were 360 acres of coffee, about one third of it irrigated.

In 1908 no crops had been proved in this area. My father and brothers tried everything they could think of including wheat, potatoes, cattle and sheep. Disease, thefts and lions played havoc with the cattle and sheep, there was no market for the potatoes when they were ready, and wheat just did not do at all. It was a hard struggle to make ends meet and for several years we only managed to exist by selling portions of the original 10 000 acre farm to other would-be settlers.

Despite all the hardships Mother's courage never failed, and soon after 1910 she managed to establish a small herd of native cows. They produced enough milk for her to start a butter trade with the Europeans living in Parklands. The only means of transport then was a donkey wagon which went to Nairobi every two months and took two days each way. Obviously this could not be used to take the butter, and my mother engaged a Kikuyu who carried 40 lb. of it on his head, and came back the same day bringing the household groceries. For this he was paid 50 cents.

We lived cheaply then with plenty of birds and buck for the pot and an abundant supply of vegetables from my mother's garden. This was down on the banks of the Ndarugu River, some two miles from the homestead.

She worked down there alone most days, or with one of us younger children as a companion. She planted many kinds of fruit trees and some of them did extremely well, so that in due course she was able to supply the surrounding farmers with pawpaws, mangoes, bananas, loquats, oranges and lemons. Every Friday morning there would be a queue of Africans waiting with their *kikapus* and these were filled at 2/- each.

My mother was the true founder of the pineapple industry. In 1905 her son-in-law, Herbert Cowie, went to live in Nairobi where he had a large garden. He imported many kinds of fruit from South Africa, pineapple suckers among them. Probably these originated in Florida. They didn't seem to thrive, so Herbert Cowrie uprooted them and threw them over his garden fence.

My mother had shown interest from the start in these pineapples, and was horrified to hear that they had been thrown away. She saddled her donkey, inspanned the wagon, went to Nairobi and collected the cast-away suckers. Today, apart from some grown by Libby, McNeal and Libby, it is thought that those original 200 suckers imported, thrown out and rescued, are the parents of every smooth-skinned pineapple in Kenya.

Under her care the cast-offs thrived, we increased our acreage, and when coffee prices slumped so disastrously, they provided our only income. Without them we could never have held on to the farm. They paid for our first tractor, and in 1927 for Mother's first real holiday.

Our usual mode of transport to Nairobi was by donkey cart. We used to leave in a small wagon pulled by about ten donkeys. It was customary to spend the night in the forest just beyond the Kamiti River, and reach Nairobi by mid-morning. This trip was usually biannual. After an enterprising business opened at Ruiru, people were able to buy dry goods at the Scots Town Stores.

The opening of a branch line to Thika in 1912, called the Thika Tramway, was a great event. A passenger could board the train at any spot between Nairobi and Thika by standing on the rail and holding up his hand. Similarly a passenger could inform the driver at Nairobi Station at what mileage and telegraph post he wanted to alight and the train would stop for him.

Twice a week, Monday and Friday, a farmers' train was run from Thika to Nairobi and back. Many farmers used to give Mr Good, the permanent guard of the train, their cheques, and when the train returned in the evening Mr Good used to hand out bags of money all along the line. Everything went into the carriages. Lizzie Barnes of the Scots Town Stores always had bags of flour, potatoes, onions, etc., in the carriage, her goods stacked in one, whilst she travelled in another compartment. One passenger carried a 20-foot length of four-inch piping tied to the running board of the carriage.

Mother died in 1941 – before the opening of the canning factory at Thika (1950) which now takes thousands of tons of pines, grown mainly by Africans, from within a radius of 50 miles. I believe it is the second largest in Africa.

Civic Progress

by Godwin Wachira

One of Thika's oldest relics is a fig tree which, it is claimed, was flourishing more than 100 years ago. One of our philosophers who lived in Kikuyuland at the turn of the last century, Mugo wa Kibiru, is believed to have prophesied that before the fig tree died, Africans would have obtained their freedom. Throughout the colonial administration this prophecy was kept alive and the tree, which could be seen by the Nairobi-Nyeri road turn-off to Thika township, died after independence, defying all the supports and nursing which it had received during colonial days.

The first business to be opened in Thika was a shop started by Jamal Hirji on the site of the present Blue Posts Hotel. This was in 1906 when Thika was only a collection of a few small huts. Before long other traders followed him. On 15 March 1924 Thika was gazetted a township. On 5 July 1963 it became a fully-fledged municipality.

Lorries wait to offload the wattle bark through which Thika's growth began

By 1967 there were nine large industries in the town, employing more than 5000 people. There is now a 100-bed hospital, a cinema, two hotels, six primary schools, two secondary schools and one technical high school. There is a children's home and a new secondary school for the blind, to supplement the oldest primary blind school in the country. There is also a primary school for cripples. All these special schools are run by the Salvation Army.

Rugby football

Thika claims the honour of starting Rugby in Kenya in 1923. One Saturday a match was scheduled for the afternoon. Mr Dennis Perry went down that morning to get the ground in order and found a rhino in the middle of the field. He ran back for his gun, shot the rhino, and then solved the problem of removing the carcase by towing it off the field with a team of oxen. The match was held without further incident.

A 1966 warning by Thika Municipal Council

Chickens that are roaming within the Municipal housing estates will
be confiscated by the council and given free to the Council's children's
home.

Kitimuru 1912 to 1920

by Nellie Grant

We bought 500 acres at Thika from Jim Elkington. It was part of a 5000 acre
block, stretching from the edge of the Kikuyu land unit to the Blue Posts Hotel and
lying between the Thika and Chania Rivers, that had been given to him by a Mr
Wyndham as a token of gratitude for the treatment of a poisoned foot by Mrs
Elkington. We paid £5 an acre, considered by earlier buyers to be exorbitant. It
was all under bush and forest and there were, of course, no roads.

After living for some time in the usual thatched *banda* made of bundles of dry
grass, with an earth floor – a paradise for white ants, if for no one else – we
embarked on the building of a real stone house. For this we engaged a
builder/contractor from Nairobi who cast envious eyes on a small, rather
battered Standard car which we had proudly bought, only to find that lack of
roads made its use extremely limited. The builder's finances were, like our own,
somewhat shaky, but he was able to reassure clients by talking business on the
steps of his bank, saying: 'I have the Bank of India behind me.' He took over the
car for a good round sum in lieu of cash as part payment for his work.

After a while polo was started at Makuyu, 16 miles away, by Mervyn Ridley
and Randall Swift. (Everyone had ponies to ride so there was no problem of
expensive mounts.) Makuyu always had a galaxy of 'pupils' – young men straight
from England, many of them horse and hunting minded, who paid satisfactory
sums to their employer for their training, not the other way round. On Saturday
afternoons we used to ride the 16 miles, mostly across country, for a game of polo
that evening. Sunday mornings were given over to hunting – jackal if the fates
were kind, small buck if they were not. The hounds had also been known to tree a
leopard, and to be wounded by porcupines which shot their quills in the hounds'
faces. On Sunday evening we rode back, all on the same ponies.

We were busy getting in our first 50 acres of coffee. Little was known about
coffee growing, but hopes ran high. To clear the land of bush, remove the tree-
stumps, and plough and plant, a great deal of hard labour was necessary. We
made coffee nurseries down by the river, 200 feet below the house, as constant
watering was essential, and then planted out the seedlings in the land we had
prepared. I remember writing to my sister to say I had planted 2000 trees that
week. She replied, 'What a wonder you are – 18 hollyhocks nearly killed me!' It
was so easy to slip into the way of saying one had done something, meaning one
had supervised it.

For some time after the First World War there was no central factory for
curing coffee, so some planters built their own. On one occasion when Jos was

away and I was supervising the drying of a batch of coffee, I made a cosy nest for myself among some sacks and wrote my Christmas letters, until the indicator on the drier should show that the right degree of dryness had been reached. This took a long time and I got bored. I noticed that the whole factory was in a mess and the floors needed to be swept, so I got some Africans with brooms to have a real blitz on it. All the coffee lying around was put into sacks. Now the problem arose of how to mark the sacks, because obviously our own mark could not be used for such rubbish. So I decided on M.U.M. for 'messed up muck' or 'Mum's the word'. When the monthly returns arrived from the selling agents in London, M.U.M. headed the list for selling price. There was great curiosity on the part of growers – 'Whose mark is this? Who is this new fellow M.U.M.?' But we kept mum.

One Sunday we decided to attend a church service to be held by a visiting parson at the Blue Posts Hotel. I donned a spotless white linen dress and tidied up generally. We were about to start when an African – unknown to us – arrived with the forefinger of his right hand dangling by a thread of skin. There had been some rock-blasting going on and he thought he would take home a detonator or two, with this result. I was somewhat baffled as to procedure but finally seized the dangling bit, popped everything into a solution of permanganate of potash and strapped the two bits of finger together. They joined up and, after a few dressings, he once more had a perfectly good forefinger. But alas for my spotless white go-to-meeting outfit, all bloodstained. No church today.

On another occasion I was called to a woman's hut where she had just given birth and was having a terrible haemorrhage. I pushed her feet into the grass roof of her hut well above her head, and told everyone to leave her like that till I came back and on no account to give her anything to eat or drink. I went away, and some crisis – I forgot what – occurred to distract me. I returned, I'm horrified to think how many hours later, to find my instructions had been strictly obeyed. She was there just as I had left her – and complete recovery ensued. Burns were awful, especially on babies who fell into the huts' fires. By modern practice we did all the wrong things, but as far as I remember never lost a baby.

As for honesty: mule carts stood about in Nairobi loaded with food and unattended, ox-wagons carrying produce and stores arrived intact. Box-body cars had no lock-up devices. But once, in 1915, I went to Nairobi and with great difficulty persuaded the bank manager to let me draw out £50 in rupees to pay the wages. When I got back to the farm about dusk, I was called off to some *shauri* and left the bag of rupees in the car. I returned to lock it up – no bag. Darkness was creeping on and I knew that, once night fell, the rupees would be well on their way to some Kikuyu village and gone forever. I summoned everyone and said unless I got the bag back in half an hour I would set alight every hut on the farm (strictly illegal, of course). Before the half-hour was up a somewhat sheepish gentleman arrived with the bag of rupees, saying he had found it under the sitting turkey. 'Oh, the naughty bird', I said, but gave him no reward.

SIX
MAKUYU AND MITUBIRI

Mount Kenya

Makuyu is a Kikuyu word for fig tree; the place is 15 miles from Thika, and so dominated by Mount Kenya that nearly every house faces the mountain. Below the Ithanga Hills lie the False Ithangas, with Fools' Valley in between. Good coffee grows on the False Ithangas and there is usually a cool breeze. Although there are several streams and rivers, most people have to depend on dams for their water supplies. The dams are mostly stocked with tilapia and bass, but they also have bilharzia so you cannot bathe in them.

The earliest European settlers were Randall Swift and Ernest Rutherfoord. They arrived in the district in 1904 and started to plant sisal in 1906 – the first to do so, commercially, in Kenya. At Punda Milia they shared a bicycle between them and when they wanted to go to Nairobi, about 50 miles, they took it in turns to ride the bicycle, the other one trotting along behind. Ernest Rutherfoord once fetched a 30-lb. fly-wheel from Nairobi on his back, against a strong head-wind. They came from Ireland where they had worked together in a brewery.

Then came Mervyn Ridley and Donald Seth Smith, who in partnership with several friends and relations founded Sisal Ltd., which was registered in 1908. Mervyn Ridley started a pack of foxhounds at Makuyu which hunted all manner of quarry over the plains.

Most of the wild game have now given place to the cultivation of coffee and sisal, but Tana Ranch is still a miniature game park. There the lions still constantly worry the cowherds and there are many species of buck, giraffe and wild pig.

Encouragement

Randall Swift recorded that he and Rutherfoord once travelled the 50 miles to Nairobi to get the advice of the Director of Agriculture and received this:

'Well, where you are at Punda Milia you are rather too high to do any good with fibres and you are too low to grow wheat or barley. Of course maize and beans would grow well with you, but then you are too far from the market. Then there is stock – that should do well, but really there are so many diseases in this country that I would not recommend that. In fact Punda Milia is one of those betwixt and between places, and I am glad I did not advise you to take up land there.'

Sisal Ltd

by A B Johansen

When I joined Sisal Ltd in 1921, the crop was still in the experimental stage and we learned as we went along. In 1932 we had the heaviest rains ever recorded. Practically all dams and bridges were washed away and the black cotton plains were under water. That year Roger Money, a local settler, decided to get married in April, the wettest month of the year.

The bride was being married from the Walker-Munros' house at Maji Kiboko, some six miles from the church (which was entirely built of sisal poles). She intended to reach the church in style, by car. But no cars could move so she had to be more or less carried most of the way. The cake and wine were sent for by runner – wader, more correctly – and the reception was held in my primitive bachelor shack, adorned only by a picture cut out of the *Daily Mirror*.

During the week the floods were at their worst, Mrs Rutherfoord chose to have her fifth daughter. The other four had all been born on the farm with the help of a midwife, a friend of the family called Mrs Scott, who later founded the Bydand Nursing Home in Nairobi. This time she got as far as Thika all right, by train, but after that the car laid on to meet her had to be pulled by oxen through the mud, and she had to wade a flooded river bounding the estate. Despite all these adventures she arrived on time and so did the baby.

That same week a European police inspector from Fort Hall arrived at my house at six in the evening on foot, accompanied by one of our local settlers who had been arrested for some offence or other. The motor cycle and sidecar in which they had been travelling had been abandoned in the mud several miles back and I had no option but to offer them a shake-down for the night. So I gave them whisky and a good dinner and put up two camp beds in my living room. Prisoner and escort slept there peacefully side by side.

Dr Sequeira, an eminent doctor from Harley Street, retired and bought a farm in our district. Mrs Sequeira was a very lively person and loved entertaining. On one occasion she organized a fête in her garden in aid of charity. She had us all, young and old, rehearsing for weeks dancing round the Maypole. On the big day we all dressed up in fancy costumes and danced round the Maypole in the sunshine, to music provided by the Doctor playing the piano and Eric Burrows playing a violin he hadn't touched for 20 years. *Greensleeves* was sung by a young man called Gledhill. It was a splendid show.

A dinner party

by N Harraway

I came to live at Makuyu in 1931. I remember well my first dinner party. I went down to the plains to find something to eat, and met a Greater Bustard. I had been told that Lesser Bustard were very good eating so I supposed the Greater would be equally good, and better for my party as there was more of it. So I shot him and lugged him on to the saddle in front of me and carried him home. When I took him into the kitchen my hopes were shattered, as he wouldn't begin to go into the oven of the old Dover stove. The cook was quite undaunted. He said he would cook him on some stones outside in a *debe*. I don't know how the cook managed, but my huge bustard turned out to be the most delicious bird.

We had a large one-roomed establishment made of mud and sisal poles, held together with wire netting and plastered inside and out, and a separate bedroom close by. We had hurricane lamps and our bathwater was carried in *debes* heated over a wood fire. We painted the inside of the house cream with huge black beams to hold up the roof, which was thatch. The floor was concrete. Now we have modern houses with water laid on and electric light. The roads are tarmac or murram, one never thinks of chains; and down on the plains the waving grasslands have gone. The zebra, ostriches and *kongoni* have gone too, and I should think a Greater Bustard is a thing of the past.

Kitito Catholic Mission

by Father R Bruno

Lt Col and Mrs Risley came to settle in the district after the First World War and bought a coffee farm between Kitito and Kakuzi. Mrs Risley, being a practising Catholic, was unhappy at being able to attend Mass no more than two or three times a year. In 1923 she wrote to Rome and asked if something could be done. As a result a Father from Fort Hall started to visit the surrounding estates to say Mass more frequently. He also opened a primary school on each estate.

In 1927 Major Hearl proposed that a mission dispensary should be built and run by a nurse nun. Father Bosca came from Nyeri to implement this idea, and within a year all buildings were completed: chapel, dispensary and staff houses. In

1945 Father Pezzoni was appointed to Kitito and under his guidance the dispensary became a hospital with a resident doctor. The primary school became an intermediate boarding school.

In 1964 a collection was started among all families in the area and a new Harambee Secondary School was built, giving education to the majority of boys and girls of the area. In 1967 a new and larger church was built which now welcomes all men of goodwill.

Coffee Seed from Aden

John Paterson, a trained horticulturist from Kew in London, walked from the coast in the 1890s to Kibwezi and worked with the mission there for some time. Later he moved on to Nairobi and Kikuyu: he was the man who brought the first coffee seed from Sheikh Othman to the Church of Scotland Mission. He then took up land at Mitubiri and planted coffee and *naartjes* on Thika Rapids Estate.

In later life he became something of a recluse. He died during the Second World War, leaving his estate to Dr Barnardo's Homes.

SEVEN

NAIVASHA, GILGIL AND THE KINANGOP

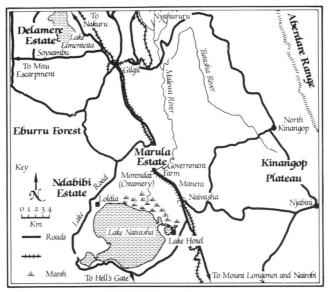

A Naivasha Notebook

by Yuilleen Hewett

(i) The scene

Naivasha is a Maasai word meaning 'rippling waters' and refers to the lake. It is one of the most beautiful of the Rift Valley lakes, edged in many places by feathery papyrus and blue water-lilies. In stormy weather the papyrus breaks off and forms floating islands which bank up to form sheltered lagoons. These prove a haven for every variety of water bird, from the huge Goliath Heron to the exquisite blue Malachite Kingfisher. The township, at an altitude of 6235 feet, is 54 miles from Nairobi.

Above Naivasha the country rises in a series of plateaux to the Kinangop mountain in the Aberdare range, whose highest peak is Satima at just over 13 000 feet. At the head of the lake is the extinct crater, Mount Longonot, rising to 9111 feet, which is ridged and runnelled by ancient lava flows. On the perpendicular red cliffs of a cleft known as Hell's Gate, Ol 'Butot in Maasai, Griffon Vultures nest, and sometimes a pair of Lammergeyer or Bearded Vultures. These birds are rare in Kenya; they are ashy-brown with tawny underparts and creamy heads, and have an immense wing-span.

Roughly nine miles down, the valley opens out into a circular bowl which is a thermal region of steam jets, erupting mud and boiling water, and the earth in many places scorches the hand. Mount Longonot itself is now an animal sanctuary and buffalo, lion, giraffe, eland, Chandler's reedbuck and klipspringer can still be seen. From there the country rises to a further escarpment, and then to the Mau plateau which forms the western wall of the Rift.

(ii) The Government Farm

By 1902 Britain was finding the Uganda Railway an expensive luxury, and the Government decided to invite white settlers to take up land in areas unpopulated, except by occasional bands of wandering Maasai, in order to establish an economy. In 1904 the embryonic Department of Agriculture set up an experimental farm at Naivasha and installed J K Hill as the first manager. Mrs Hill described their arrival:

'There were only two trains a week between Nairobi and Nakuru. The Provincial Commissioner, S S Bagge, met us at the station with *askaris*, and a wagonette drawn by four mules. We drove off along a winding track through trees, and eventually reached a corrugated iron bungalow on piles, with a barbed wire fence round it to keep out wild animals. Water was fetched daily from the Malewa River by ox-cart, and, for washing, poured into a tin bath from *debes*.

Sometimes I did not see another European woman for three months or more, but I had my lovely Bechstein piano, and as I could play and sing I passed the time away. When any musical settlers came along we had "sing-songs and jolly hops", our only entertainment.'

The Hills used to drive into Naivasha in a four-in-hand drawn by zebras, complete with hunting horn, passing through herds of plains game almost all the way. These zebra were bought by Lord Rothschild, to be driven in the London parks.

(iii) Early settlers

One of the first was J D Hopcraft. He applied for land on the west side of the lake; it had to be surveyed, and much delay was caused by the loss of the surveyor; he was taken by a python when swimming the Malewa River, and his papers went with him. The Hopcraft homestead consisted of a lion-proof stockade built round a thorn tree to protect the cattle, with a one-roomed shack adjoining for the owners. Its design was copied by most of the new arrivals. Other early comers

The Lake Hotel, Naivasha

Loldia, 1906, built by J D Hopcraft; this was the first stone house round Lake Naivasha

were H Dobbin and C B Burnell, both professional well-diggers. Safaris of Kikuyu women used to carry loads of maize, bananas, flour and beans all the way over the Aberdares to sell, to feed the labourers who were taught the use of the farm tools.

Eburru Mountain was entirely waterless but riddled with steam jets. My father, S F Smithson, discovered that if he led the steam from fumaroles into pipes it condensed, and a fairly good supply of water could be obtained. In recognition of this he was granted a tract of land by the Governor, Sir Percy Girouard.

Captain and Mrs Fey, with their two daughters Nell and Norah and their son Jim, took up land on the South Kinangop plateau, below the foothills of Mount Kinangop, in 1906, and were the first to settle there. They called their farm N'Jibini, now spelt Njabini on maps. They raised cattle, had ostriches for a while and started a sawmill. The timber was sent on ox-wagons 25 miles across the plateau and down the escarpment to the railhead at Naivasha.

(iv) Paul Rainey

One of the lake farms was sold to an American millionaire, Paul Rainey, who imported coon dogs to hunt lion. The followers were on horseback, and I became his whipper-in. We also chased and captured cheetah, to be sold to Indian rajahs for hunting buck.

Paul Rainey had a chimpanzee called Dooley. When he grew older, Dooley was measured for a suit of clothes. He used to sit on the front seat of Rainey's car, dressed in his suit and smoking a cigarette. But when he grew up, he was chained most of the time to a tree; it was said to keep him out of mischief. He became adept at loosening his chain, and even learned to pick the lock of a padlock, if he could get hold of a nail. In later life he grew savage and had to be destroyed.

(v) Trials and errors

Potatoes were one of the earliest crops, but proved a failure. Then ostrich farming was the thing. Nat Barry imported stud ostrich cocks from South Africa, and other people got huge incubators from America. But fashions changed and the ostriches were let loose to go wild again. As late as 1924 I can remember massive omelettes made from ostrich eggs – delicious. It was said that Will Powys used to bore a hole and pour out sufficient egg for his breakfast, an egg lasting three or four days.

The eggs, milk and butter which we produced were at first carried by Africans on foot to Naivasha and sold to Government officials in the *boma*. Once an African, bearing, among other things, a biscuit tin packed with eggs, was charged by a rhino and killed. Later we packed the produce into 60-lb. wooden boxes and railed it to Nairobi.

Livestock were continually dying from deadly tick-borne diseases such as East Coast Fever, Heart-water, Red-water and Anaplasmosis, and virus complaints such as Rinderpest, Anthrax, Quarter-evil and Foot-and-Mouth. Losses were heavy, and it was years before reliable vaccines and serums were found to control these evils. Present day farming is child's play compared with the endless struggle to combat disease in cattle and sheep experienced by the early settlers.

You cannot be a pioneer farmer without being an optimist, and optimism sometimes got out of hand. Powys Cobb took up land at a high altitude on top of the Mau Escarpment to grow wheat in a big way. He imported huge steam tractors, and had barges built to carry the harvested crops across the lake to the railhead at Naivasha. He had a deep ditch dug to keep out game. But when the wheat was planted, the land proved quite unsuitable. I heard that Crowned Cranes arrived in thousands to follow the planters and eat the seeds, finally breaking him financially.

The Macraes' sisal drying on the south lake shore

In the early 1920s the three McCrae brothers came to Naivasha and planted sisal on a large scale, south of the lake. At their peak they had 11 000 acres of it. The district proved unsuitable for the best quality sisal and, after many years of struggle, the McCraes finally left. Eventually Block Estates bought the land and used it to supply their hotels with eggs and poultry.

Between 1927 and 1928 the Co-operative Creamery was started at Naivasha. Lord Delamere and T Chillingworth put up much of the money. Of the large-scale farmers Lord Delamere at Manera, Sir John Ramsden at Marula and Gilbert Colville at Ndabibi were the most productive.

Dried Vegetables

The opening of a dried vegetable factory in Naivasha township by Pan African Vegetable Products Ltd provided welcome local employment. It also became an outlet for vegetables grown by farmers round the lake, and more recent settlers on the Kinangop.

Masai. 1909.
The ball of black ostrich feathers on the tip of the spear, called a "sussel" is the peace sign.

Gilgil

by Lady Eleanor Cole

When I arrived in 1916 our party, consisting of my cousin, Mrs Milne, and brother-in-law, Berkeley Cole, had ridden over from Berkeley's farm at Naro Moru. There was no passable road from Gilgil to Nairobi, only a wagon track, and of course, the railway. The station served as Post Office, and Gilgil consisted, besides this, of one Indian *duka* belonging to Nathoo Madhavji, whose descendants still had a shop in the town in 1968.

Among the first settlers were Lord Delamere, Hobson, and Galbraith Cole, who bought out Hobson and took up land as far as the slopes of Eburru. His original grant was waterless except for one bank of two small streams, but by buying out Hobson he acquired both banks, and by ploughing back all available money, he managed eventually to supply water by pipeline to the whole area of over 30 000 acres. The water of Lake Elmenteita is undrinkable by man or beast.

Farming was restricted to beef and wool production, as it was too dry for arable. Galbraith imported Merino rams from Australia, and Dr Deering brought up some ewes and rams from South Africa. The rams were crossed with Maasai ewes. All farming was supervised from horseback.

Local medical services were non-existent, the nearest doctor being in Nakuru, where a few army huts formed the nucleus of what was to become the War Memorial Hospital. One of the first wives in the district rode down the steep, rocky Dundori escarpment, the haunt of buffalo and many other wild animals, the 20 miles to Nakuru to have her first baby. Escorted by her husband with a rifle and a Maasai with a spear, she arrived safely and had a fine boy.

Lady Colville, mother of Gilbert Colville, built a small house near Gilgil Station. Passenger trains used to reach Gilgil at two in the morning for a long halt to take on wood and water, so she built the hotel in self-defence against social calls at 2 a.m.

In 1916 the plains were teeming with game of all sorts. Elephants used to come down from the forest to get salt on the shores of Elmenteita, but when settlement started and wire fences were put up their annual trekking ceased. Hippos were very plentiful in the lake up to 1951 when the lake dried up; since then only one has been seen. Rhino, ostriches and now hyena have disappeared. We still have the occasional lion and cheetah and now and then a leopard. When they molest the cattle we try to trap them and send them to the Nairobi Game Park. We have serval cats and lynx, and various species of antelope and gazelle which we preserve. There are also monkeys, baboons, hares, bat-eared foxes, jackals, ant-bears, warthog, honey badgers and sometimes buffalo, but *kongoni* and Grant's gazelle have disappeared.

When Spanish 'flu swept through the country after the First World War, most of our Africans got it. Our doctor was Dr Burkitt of Nairobi whose famous cold-water treatment for all ailments involving a high temperature was in vogue. Accordingly I held a sick parade every morning and anyone whose temperature was over 100° was stripped and douched with cold water. Everyone recovered. My house servant was so impressed with this treatment that years later, when his old father appeared to be dying and had reached the stage to be carried out of the hut for fear that he should die in it, and the hut should therefore have to be destroyed, as a parting act of mercy he poured a bucket of cold water over the old man. Instead of dying, or being eaten by hyenas, his father was alive and kicking the next morning and lived for several years after that.

South Kinangop

by Evelyn Polhill

This is a rough, high country of rolling ridges and small streams, dry for three months of the year, covered with coarse grass and bush and tongues of forest. On the western side an escarpment falls 2000 feet and forms the eastern wall of the Rift Valley.

Picking pyrethrum

About 1922 wheat growing was started on the better drained land along the tops of the ridges. At first there were heavy losses from rust, and from wild animals. A farmer would go out in the early morning to see herds of zebra or Thomson's gazelle grazing happily in his young crops. So shooting the game was, alas, imperative. Farmers who kept pigs used to boil up the meat in 40-gallon drums and add it to the pigs' rations of cereals, skim milk and potatoes. Small chat potatoes were brought by trains of donkeys many miles across the plateau from the Bamboo Forest, and sold to the pig farmers for 1/- for a 200-lb bag.

About 1936 the first pyrethrum plants to be grown on South Kinangop were established by Stanley Polhill as an experiment. The plants flourished, and founded a strain that proved particularly hardy and high-yielding, still known as the Polhill strain. Stanley supplied pyrethrum splits free of charge to any farmer who cared to come along and collect them. Many took advantage of his offer and that is how the industry was established whose exports came to earn two or three million pounds a year for the country.

Pyrethrum also gave employment to the families of the farm labourers. Picking the daisies was popular work and paid for at the rate of so much a pound. Children helped their mothers and elder sisters to fill the sacks. One small girl often brought in her own weight in flowers (74 lbs) during the day. Her load would be weighed, the amount noted and then she would be weighed herself. This caused much general merriment.

EIGHT
NAKURU

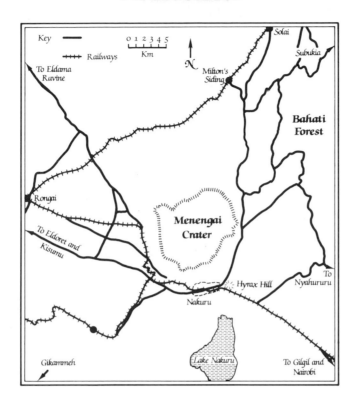

(i) Old Nakuru

There were settlers near Lake Nakuru three thousand years ago, perhaps even before that. On Hyrax Hill, a low lava ridge about three miles from the modern town, traces of prehistoric habitations were excavated in 1937 and in subsequent years by Mrs Mary Leakey. She found here stone circles and a burial ground with the remains of 19 skeletons, nine of them – those of women – accompanied by stone platters and pestles for grinding grain. (One also had two beads, and an obsidian knife.) These belong to the Neolithic Age and are believed to date back to about 1000 BC. Elsewhere on the same site Mrs Leakey found the remains of various obsidian tools such as blades, scrapers and burins (used for engraving), and also many fragments of pottery vessels, five of which have been reconstructed from the bits. A thriving community, sufficiently advanced to live in permanent stone dwellings, grow grain crops, keep livestock, make pottery vessels and bury their dead, once inhabited this settlement. What became of them no one knows.

Hyrax Hill, under the lee of the great caldera, Menengai, proved to be full of archaeological treasure. Traces of two other settlements, both much more recent, were found. The North-East Village consists of 13 sunken pit dwellings, roughly five to eight feet deep, probably shared by the people and their livestock. In them were found fragments of pottery, mostly spouted jars, as well as obsidian artefacts. This village was in occupation, probably, about the time the Tudors ruled in England. Most recent of all is an Early Iron Age settlement, not more than a few hundred years old, consisting of round dwellings built of loosely stacked boulders and smaller stones. These builders, like those before them, have vanished. Only the oldest of the sites, the Neolithic, had a burial ground.

All this can be studied in a museum-on-the-spot established in 1965 with the help of the Nakuru County Council and others, in the former home of Mrs Mary Selfe. Mrs Selfe, then a widow, worked untiringly to get Hyrax Hill scheduled as an Ancient Monument and placed under the Trustees of Kenya's National Parks. This was accomplished, and Mrs Selfe gave her house to the nation in memory of her son Timothy, shot down over Germany while serving with the RAF in the Second World War.

(ii) New Nakuru

The railway had reached Nakuru in 1900. Richard Meinertzhagen paid a visit on leave in 1902. 'I am stopping the night at the dak bungalow near the station,' he wrote in his diary: 'The dak bungalow and the station are the only buildings in the place.'

The town's official birthday is 28 January 1904, when an area 'within a circle having a radius of one mile from the main entrance to the railway station' was proclaimed to be a township.

The Maasai called it 'the place where the cows won't eat grass'. It was an arid, windswept stretch of plain between Lake Nakuru and Menengai, where soda-dust from the lake shore was apt to settle, and had no human inhabitants at all. There were no signs of Maasai manyattas. When European cattle were introduced, they suffered from a wasting disease which was called Nakuruitis, and in 1926 scientists from Aberdeen in Scotland found the cause to be a deficiency of iron in the pastures.

Pioneer Mary

Like other districts, Nakuru had its well-known characters. One was Pioneer Mary: an Irishwoman who came from Australia via South Africa, and with her husband, John Walsh, trekked with the railway as it wound its way up-country. None of her children lived. A sturdy, fiery and determined character, she kept order amongst the railway labour force with her rhino-hide whip. She also made good pies and bread, at first in a tent, then in a bakery on the site of the present Eros cinema.

On one occasion Archibald Buchan-Sydserff, a railway engineer known as

Top: Menengai, with pyrethrum in foreground

Bottom: the end of the line, taken at the turn of the century when Nakuru was still railhead

Bwana Simba, had been out all day in the bush at the height of the hot dry season, surveying towards Rongai. Weary and hungry, he was making his way back to his camp at Nakuru, looking forward to one of Mary's fresh hot loaves, a roast guinea-fowl, and a good long rest on his camp-bed. Suddenly an agitated African jumped out of the bush and barred his path.

'Return at once, Bwana Simba,' he cried. 'Memsahib Kiboko is calling for you! Quickly, come!'

Pioneer Mary was on the rampage, all ready to thrash him with her rhino-hide whip. His labourers, she claimed, had stolen sheets of corrugated iron from her ovens. Bwana Simba had to sleep out in the bush that night, supperless and weary. Nobody dared face Pioneer Mary when she was in a really good old-fashioned Irish temper. She lies buried in Nairobi Cemetery with her husband John at her side.

Builders and bakers

Amongst the earliest European builders were the Speke brothers, who arrived in 1912. They made bricks by hand from red earth at Rongai, and transported them by hand-cart to Nakuru.

Bullock wagons rumbling through the main street caused a terrific dust, and in the rains churned the surface into a quagmire. When cloud-bursts occurred over Menengai, before trees were planted on its crest, water would come tumbling down the lava furrows and form a lake in the earth road. Houses were raised on wooden piles and had verandahs with wooden steps leading up to them. These were expected to keep out the flood water and silt, and prevent snakes from entering. Many housewives planted geraniums round their doorways, believing that the strong smell repelled puff-adders, which frequently made their way into houses built at ground level. Sometimes monkeys came in at night to plunder the larders.

One of the first stone houses was built for Bwana Simba in what was then Delamere Avenue. He insisted that tiles should be cemented into the wall, each one bearing a footprint. There was the imprint of his tame ostrich, those of lion, hippo, rhino and giraffe. The last was the print of the tiny Pike baby's foot. It is still embedded in the wall opposite the Nakuru Athletic Club.

During the First World War Nakuru Racecourse became an army convalescent camp. The Padre asked Mrs Albert Speke if she would make some cakes for their canteen. Albert was away at the war. Although dismayed at the thought of making cakes for 200 men on a No. 9 Dover stove, Mrs Speke agreed. Before the camp closed down she was making close on 2000 cakes a day. When Albert returned he built a brick oven and a bakehouse in Lake Road. Their three daughters used to push a hand-cart full of freshly baked loaves up to the railway station every morning before going to school.

That was the start of Speke's Bakery.

Gikammeh

by Nellie Grant

I called this farm, 1000 acres on the slopes of the Mau, by the Kikuyu word for tree hyrax, as they shrieked all night in the lovely forest which then (1923) surrounded the tiny wood-and-iron bungalow built by the first owner when the land was alienated in 1912. My nearest neighbour was Tom Petrie, who came out from Scotland in 1911. He promised to meet me at Njoro Station with a small ox-cart when I arrived from Thika with three dachshunds, two Siamese cats, camping equipment and a lot of packages. My husband was in the throes of selling our coffee plantation at Thika, and joined me some time later when the sale was complete. I was also met, much to my surprise, by six of our Kikuyu employees from Thika who, without saying a word, had gone ahead so as to be first on the spot to ask for shambas on the new farm. Among them was dear old Njombo, who was immediately appointed headman. So I had an unexpected nucleus of a labour force with which to embark on clearing some of the forest.

I found the little house full of bags of maize. It had been used as a store, but Tom Petrie had cleared one room for me, 14 feet by 14 feet, minus doors, window glass or flooring. While I was measuring the floor for boards I found myself suddenly

Top: Mrs Aubrey's house, March 1914

Bottom: Trek oxen outspanning in main street of Nakuru

unable to rise. I managed to get myself into a chair and remained there till next day, when a pony was brought to the verandah and I was heaved on board. I rode three miles along a forest track to my other neighbours, the Lindstroms, recently arrived from Sweden. Ingrid Lindstrom gave me a good rubbing and eventually mobility was restored.

Gikammeh, at 7800 feet, was mixed farming land. But first it had to be cleared. All the good timber had already been removed by Kikuyu squatters, but the enormous stumps remained underground. It all had to be done by hand, and by oxen dragging chains, and was terribly costly in labour. The ploughs kept on hitting hidden stumps for years. We grew reasonable crops of maize and cattle fodder and installed a dip for the cattle, essential because of East Coast Fever. There was also redwater, and we had an outbreak of rinderpest, brought by buffalo. There were plenty of them in the forest, and also leopards, which were a constant menace to the dogs.

The largest farm near me was Larmudiac, owned by 'Black Harries'. He and his wife had come from Wales via South-West Africa. He had a large black beard, and was immensely strong. He was said once to have pulled a wounded leopard backwards out of a bush by its tail, and finished it off by a blow on the head with his fist. One day I was at the cattle dip and we were having trouble putting some young stock through. Black Harries, who was passing, came to help and picked up a three-quarters-grown steer which had got the wrong way round in the dip; he lifted it right off its feet, swung it round to face the right way and pushed it in.

He had a passion for horses, and let them roam freely over his many acres, breeding as they wished; he never gelded them, and they built up to enormous numbers. Nor did he feed them either, and in times of drought they became half-starved or did starve, and their skeletons lay mouldering (and stinking) in the bush. Nor were they broken in.

The Harries lived in considerable squalor, by choice rather than necessity. Huge savage dogs set on visitors arriving at their house, or large hut, which seemed to be ringed by bones. And then inside you found a long, genuine oak refectory table and about 16 good Chippendale chairs. At one end Black Harries would be carving a colossal joint, at the other Mrs Harries would be disembowelling several fowls. You might have to push some Muscovy ducks off the Chippendale chairs. There was dirt everywhere, especially in the kitchen. The bedroom was a rondavel taken up by the marital bed and by a large incubator next to it. A tarpaulin had been stretched under the thatch to keep the incubator, not the Harries, dry.

No one could have presented a greater contrast than my other neighbours, the Lindstroms, as mild and gentle as the Harries were tough. Fish, as he was always called, from his African nickname Samaki (they thought he looked like one), had been a cavalry officer in Sweden, and in Kenya he took up part-time big-game hunting, and managing other people's farms, to help their finances, tightly stretched by developing their land. They had four small children, and a number of Scandinavian relations in other parts of Kenya and Tanganyika (as it was then), and gave wonderful Scandinavian parties when there was a birthday, wedding, anniversary or other occasion that called for celebration. Their hospitality was a by-word, and the Africans loved them dearly, partly perhaps because they were allowed to do more or less as they liked.

Loyalty to friends was always a strong point. One of their friends was 'Blix', Baron von Blixen, ex-husband of Tania (Karen) Blixen and one of the leading big-game hunters of the era. Despite his success as a hunter, but perhaps partly because of it in other fields (i.e. ladies, not lions), he was sometimes on the run from creditors. He would seek refuge at the Lindstroms', and Fish once diverted all his ploughing gear to making a dead-straight road, or track – normally roads were made to zig-zag up and down the hills – from their house to the Njoro road, about two miles, so that advancing creditors could be seen in good time, and Blix escape into the forest at the back of the farm. At the first onset of the rains the road, so-called, became completely impassable, thus making Blix, once there, even more secure.

In another direction a rich American from Boston, Billy Sewall, had a large house built in the Californian style by the fashionable architect of the day, a pupil of Sir Herbert Baker's called Hoogterp. With its patios and large verandahs, at 7000 feet it proved bitterly cold. But the house, full of beautiful furniture, was impeccably maintained by two Chinese servants Billy had installed. They seemed to speak no English, had no families with them and were wonderful servants. All three of them, Billy and the two Chinese, dressed for dinner in rich silk kimonos, and looked rather alike, so sometimes it was hard to know who was greeting you on arrival. The Chinese had brought their coffins with them in order to be sent back to China should they die abroad.

Nakuru School (i)

by Anne Walshe

Nakuru school, 1924

'High above the dusty highway
Where the creaking wagons go,
With a canopy of deepest blue above,
In a circle of the mountains,
With a placid lake below,
Stands the school we shall remember with our love.'

This was the school song which the children were singing when I arrived to teach in Nakuru School, on Thinking Day, 1934. Swarms of Girl Guides and Brownies greeted me.

Miss Dorothy Keeling, the Guide Captain, had kindly helped to collect my cabin-trunk at the old ramshackle wooden railway station opposite Nakuru Hotel (now the Midland). The Wild West appearance of the station and hotel terrified me. I could imagine cowboys riding up to the wooden hitching-posts, tethering their mustangs, and shooting it out. I didn't unpack my trunk for six months, saving my fare to return to Ireland.

However, we did have a motor-car to get to the school, two miles up on the slopes of Menengai. It stalled half-way up the hill. The Guides had to push it to the top.

The school was an odd medley of buildings. Where the swimming pool now stands was a huddle of wood and corrugated-iron dwellings in which the staff, including Mrs Cameron, the Senior Mistress, and Miss Zoe Goodwyn, the Music Mistress, were housed. My furniture consisted of a table, a Morris chair, an iron bedstead, a tin bath with handles, and an enamel chamberpot. Beneath the bath was a hole in the wooden floor. Bees were busily making honeycombs inside the dark wooden walls, and the boards of the floor were full of fleas. A hurricane lamp served for lighting. Cooking had to be done outside on a wood fire. When it rained, a Luo servant kindly cooked my food over a charcoal heater in his little round grass-thatched wattle-and-daub hut. I have heard new teachers arriving in Kenya on two-year contracts complaining about their living quarters. I wish they could have seen mine, 34 years ago.

The main building, designed by Sir Herbert Baker, was comparatively recent (1933) and greatly admired. But the five new dormitories were strictly for the boys. The girls slept in primitive wooden buildings, where their refectory is today.

Children seemed more enterprising in those days. One morning, only the girls appeared in the school hall for prayers. Not until mid-day were the boys discovered, at Reggie Holmes' snake-park down by the Hippo Pool. They had deserted in a body, intending to live the rest of their lives on the lake shores, shooting buck and guinea-fowl for food. Well, many of them got DFCs or DSOs with the RAF or Army in the Second World War.

Nakuru School (ii)

In the late 1950s a new school was built in the grounds of the old, to take boys of all races through to Sixth Form standard. It was called after Lord Francis Scott, in memory of the much-loved early settler of Deloraine, Rongai, who did so much to build up farming in the country. The girls took over the whole of the previous building as a High School of their own, and an entirely new primary school was built, called after Lord Lugard.

All these separate establishments were later brought into one boarding school, for both boys and girls of all races, with the help of American technical aid and with Mr Ken Penn as the first headmaster.

NINE
SUBUKIA AND SOLAI

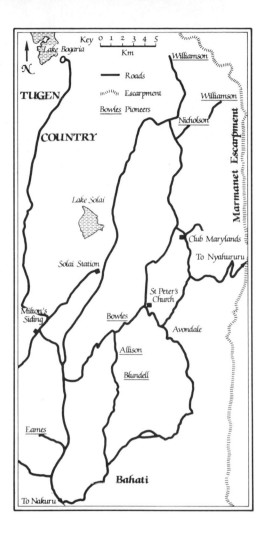

The Maasai, who used to drive their cattle down the Marmanet Escarpment when grazing on Laikipia failed, called the Subukia valley, Ol Momoi Sidai – the beautiful place. Probably its present name derives from their word for buffalo – sabuk. In 1911 they were moved away from Laikipia to join their brethren round Narok, so the valley was uninhabited when the first settlers came. This was not until 1919 to 1920, when the Soldier Settlement Scheme was launched after the First World War.

Count Teleki and Lieutenant von Höhnel were the first Europeans to see Subukia. In November 1887 they camped in 'a pretty valley' at 7287 feet. Thence they 'proceeded to the adjacent valley of Solai, at whose north-western end lies

Central Subukia looking north

Lake Hannington (now Bogoria), hidden away in a little rift valley of its own.' (Sir Harry Johnstone)

In January 1888 Lake Hannington was quite dry, and von Höhnel saw clouds of dust above it raised by flocks of ostriches. Normally, aquatic birds live here in thousands, and Sir Harry Johnstone estimated that in 1900 there were 'close on a million flamingoes'.

The first European to take up land in Solai was Frank Watkins, in 1909, followed in 1910 by Frank Baillie and in 1911 by the two brothers, 'Long' and 'Short' Eames. By 1928 Solai had 26 landowners with 15 000 acres under cultivation, mainly maize with a little coffee, and 54 000 acres of grazing.

Subukia had by then 38 landowners; in all, 85 Europeans, including 19 children. (In 1920 there were only ten Europeans.) Already there was a Country Club with 32 members. The price of land was £2 to £5 per acre, and a man of 'the right type', according to the Subukia Farmers' Association, ought to be able to make good on a capital of £1000.

An Appreciation

by Sir Michael Blundell

The Subukia Valley nestles in the broken folds of the eastern wall of the Rift Valley, falling from 8000 feet above sea level to rough hills at 5000 feet which descend to Lake Bogoria. Because of its remoteness the early waves of European settlers passed it by. The deep forest, the steep hills which barred entry and the high rainfall, preserved its seclusion. It was not until the early 1920s that the first homesteads began to be built and land began to be cleared for crops.

As late as 1928 the whole valley from the top of the National Farm, Avondale, to the edge of Marylands Estates, was thick deep forest, the haunt of innumerable buffalo, herds of elephant, leopards, bushbuck and troops of Sykes and Colobus monkeys. This grey-green forest, like a mixture of sage and jade, stretched for 20 miles southwards. At intervals clearings of purple earth showed up among the trees, and here and there arose columns of smoke from the smouldering fires of charcoal-burners.

Early in the depression of the thirties, because of its distance from the railway, and abominable roads, Subukia was forced out of maize and other arable crops into dairying and pigs. Many of the early farmers had a very thin time, living as best they could on their meagre cream and bacon factory cheques, and such credit as they could muster. Babu Ram, whose duka was one of the two in the valley, helped many a landowner through.

Every Sunday the hard-pressed farmers emerged from the valley and the hills, wherever they were tucked away, and were wonderfully entertained by the Ecksteins, who came in 1924 to Marylands Estates. Herman would take the church service, Molly played the piano and the rest of us would sing. Great Danes – as many as 20 – would stalk about during meals, and the house, originally made of planks of greenheart, was gradually extended so that neighbours could stay the night. Through drought and disasters – one year the piggery caught fire and all the pigs were killed – the Ecksteins provided a family oasis for people old and young.

It must be remembered that during the rains movement on the roads was hazardous and time-consuming. The road down to Milton's Siding was not built until 1928, and half way up, near the Ol Donyo Mara coffee, was a great hazard called 'Black Bottom' in which many a car and lorry foundered.

An early settler once said, 'It may be a fools' paradise, or so I'm told, but at least it *is* paradise.'

Such is Subukia.

Left: Sir Michael Blundell's first house in Solai, 1925. Right: his later house in Subukia

Gun-carriage

Subukia Rifle Club (1932 to 1939) had a number of women members, one of whom was old Mrs McKenzie. She used to come in her Model T Ford to shoot but the Ford no longer had an engine but was pulled by six donkeys.

White Rocks Farm

by Mrs Margaret Nicholson

We bought 3000 acres in 1929 from Willie Allison, and my husband found another farm, on the Subukia River, for his parents. They arrived early in 1930. Life was hard indeed for them that first year. They planted 120 acres for maize; their crop was good, but fetched only 6/- a bag (200 lbs), whereas the previous year the price had been 10/-. Luckily my mother-in-law was a woman of grit and determination. She started poultry, made a beautiful garden, and planted the swamp in vegetables and fruit trees – invaluable in the next three years when we all had to live off the farms or starve.

In 1931 our crops were planted, using oxen, as the tractor cost too much to run, and then came the locusts. They came in their hordes, and everything was eaten flat overnight. We made smoky fires round the shambas and all the labour turned out to shout and bang on *debes*, but nothing would move a swarm which had decided to settle for the night. The labourers would fill their *debes* with locusts to make a meal for themselves. The grass was nibbled down till there was nothing left but red soil which was so poisoned that it took two years to grow grass again. The hoppers swarmed over the ground like a large moving carpet and once went straight through the house, up the mud walls and down the other side, eating all the curtains and rugs on their way. We put down poison bait near the river; the hoppers ate it and went into the water, making the river a solid black mass of dead bodies.

The locusts came again in 1932 and we had no crops for sale either year, no grass for the cattle, and things were in a very bad way. We still met at each other's houses offering home-grown coffee and home-made ginger beer for drinks, and took anything possible for sale in Nakuru. We ran a butchery on the farm.

After the locusts came the drought, and what little maize there was fetched only 5/- a bag. Now the depression really set in, and there was no alternative but to abandon the farm until we had some capital to develop it. So for the next ten years the farm lay idle.

My husband was lucky enough to get a job as manager for £12 a month, until he was called up in 1940. I went back to teaching. In 1943 my husband was released to go back to the farm and try to get production going. I was not released until 1946. By now, my husband had got together a little capital, £3000, and

Top: borehole pump on White Rocks Farm made from an old tractor, railway line and cart wheels

Middle: Tom and Margaret's first car – Box-body Chevrolet

Bottom: early settlers in Solai

there was a prisoner-of-war camp on our land, clearing bush for tsetse-fly control, so he was able to draw on some Italian labour.

He found barely a sign left of previous habitation. The house and stores had fallen down and all that remained was the cattle dip and a tiny stone dairy. The fruit trees in the swamp garden and a few flowers amongst the weeds in the old house garden were all that was left to tell the story of those hard and heart-breaking early years.

With the help of the Italians we built a mud house, so that all available labour could plough ready for planting. We built pig-sties and stores, and bought more cattle, gradually grading up the native stock with the use of various types of bull – Sahiwal, Red Poll, Ayrshire and Friesian; but we found it necessary to go back to the Boran, because of disease.

Now we run 1000 head of cattle, mostly for the Meat Commission. We grow maize, and crops for feedstuffs, with some barley and wheat, and grow practically all the food for our pigs. We have sunk three boreholes and put in a ram, cleared a lot of bush, fenced paddocks, and planted 80 acres of coffee. We have made a new garden from the bush, kept poultry and rabbits, brought up a family, doctored the sick, kept the accounts, and in addition to the usual chores I ran the Rift Valley Correspondence Course for teaching children in their homes from 1946 to 1950, in partnership with another Subukia farmer's wife, Mrs Beverley.

We employ about 100 Africans whose wives help as casual labour. They all get shambas to grow their own crops, have access to a good water supply, and there is a flourishing school on the farm built by us, now taken over by the Nakuru County Council. This is what we have accomplished and there is still much to do. We hope to hand on White Rocks Farm in good heart to our successors.

Distressing Incidents

(i) One day Terry Fitzgerald of Solai stumbled on a large python, and found himself wrapped round and round in its coils. There was no one he could call on for help. He managed to get hold of the reptile's jaw and tried to break its neck. It seemed a very long time indeed, while he felt himself more tightly squeezed and growing weaker, before he felt its backbone snap and the blessed relief as the coils relaxed. His hand was badly lacerated by the snake's teeth and he was bruised all over, but he escaped with his life.

by Dr Roger Bowles

(ii) Gendin Farm was plagued by marauding baboons. I had read an article in a South African paper on how to discourage them. I trapped a large dog baboon, painted him pillar-box red, tied a cow-bell round his neck and released him. Then I caught a bitch baboon and painted her green, and also released her. Early next morning there they were – two large baboons, red and green, sitting together on a prominent rocky outcrop. Behind them was the largest pack of baboons I had ever seen, looking like an expectant audience. I fired a shot over the heads of the two harlequins. Off they went, the bell tinkling, followed by the rest of the pack. That rid the district of baboons.

More than a year later a neighbour was riding home from a late Sunday lunch with some hospitable friends, when suddenly he saw a scarlet baboon crossing his path, ringing a bell. 'I've got 'em!' he yelled, and galloped home. I visited him in the Nakuru War Memorial Hospital were he was under observation for *delirium tremens*, and was able to convince a sceptical doctor that his patient's story was a true one.

by Fritz Freyburg

(iii) In 1929 my hut on the old '35' farm had been inhabited by Colonel Lean's manager, who had shared it with his wife and a python. This python was the wife's pet, and seemed to dislike the husband intensely. The python shared the wife's bed and the husband didn't dare go near her. There came a time when she had to go to England for several months. She put the python in a comfortable cage and made her husband promise, by all he held dear, to care for it tenderly during her absence. For days after her departure the poor fellow was tormented. What should he do? Old Colonel Lean was in no doubt. 'If you're half a man, shoot the damned thing.' At last the manager poked a shotgun into the cage and blew its head off. When his wife returned, everyone had been coached to tell the same story. The python had pined away and died from a broken heart during its mistress's absence.

by R Williamson

(iv) In the early days one of our difficulties was to overcome an African custom of putting a sick person, believed to be dying, outside the hut at night, as a rule to be eaten by hyenas. It was believed that if anyone died inside, the hut would be contaminated and have to be destroyed. Our headman came to me and said that one of the men and his wife were most perturbed because a sick child who had been put outside had crawled back into the hut three nights in succession. The father reluctantly brought the unfortunate little thing to me and I found that she was suffering from malaria and pneumonia following exposure. I treated her accordingly, and she made a complete recovery.

The Admiral, part 1

by PRW

(v) In 1925 there was very heavy rain, and one day no less than seven cars were stuck on an extremely bad patch of mud. Admiral Blunt volunteered to try and find a diversion and so took off into the *bundu*. After waiting for some time we thought we had better go and find out what had happened, but no trace of the Admiral, his wife or his car was to be seen. It eventually transpired that they had all disappeared into a newly formed *donga* and the bush had closed over the car, leaving no sign.

The Admiral, part 2

(vi) On another occasion the Admiral, travelling with his wife from Solai to Nakuru in his box-body Model T Ford, hit a pothole with such impact that not only did his good lady hit the roof, but her head went straight through it. The plywood then, as plywood will, closed round her neck and nothing that the Admiral could do would release her. As the vehicle was also stuck in the mud, there was nothing for it but to walk to Nakuru for help. As the Admiral trudged on it began to rain. The road surface became muddier and muddier. By the time he reached Nakuru he was exhausted, soaked, and covered in mud. His friends rallied round him. A little drink would do him a power of good. Two little drinks . . . Several hours later someone asked the Admiral how his missus was. It was the first time he had given the poor woman a thought.

by D. M. S. Allison

(vii) An earthquake shook Subukia in January 1928. One farmer's wife was in her bath at the time and a large hole appeared in the wall. She shouted for help and the young manager, who was passing, pulled her through the gap. She was a very beautiful woman and afterwards his friends teased him unmercifully and asked him what she looked like. His reply of 'I couldn't see, she was too muddy' took some time to live down.

A button factory

Stuart Allison built a small factory near Lake Solai in 1959 for making buttons. He installed a Turkish manager. After a lot of experimenting he had chosen three raw materials – coconut shells, *leleshwa* roots, and doum-palm nuts. The first two were used chiefly for large coat buttons, which were most attractive. Doum-palm nuts were found to be exceedingly hard, and to take dyes well. Segments were cut from the outsides of the nuts and used to make small coat and trouser buttons. These nuts came down from the Northern Province via Kapenguria to Kitale, where Stuart collected them. All went well, and orders came in thick and fast from all over Africa. Then in 1961 the floods came. Doum-palm are found near river-beds and the inundated country completely disrupted transport. Other nuts were brought from Lamu, but soon floods hit the coast and these failed too. The factory had to close down.

The first settler in Subukia

by Mrs Vera Williamson

My husband came out under the Soldier Settler Scheme and reached the land he had selected, travelling in a Scotch cart drawn by oxen, on New Year's Day 1920. We were married in Mombasa in March 1923. There were only three other European women in Subukia then. Our farm was forty miles from Nakuru, and it took an African four or five days to fetch the mail; he would also bring money from the bank with never a cent missing.

Wild animals were a great trial to us then. We were struggling to create a farm from the bush and had little money to spare for replacing stock taken by lion or leopard, or maize trampled by buffalo. Once, when Bill was out on the farm, an African came running to say that some buffalo had got in among the cattle and would I get a gun and drive them off. I snatched a rifle and ammunition and set off, clad of course in high boots against snakes, and my sun-helmet. On arrival at the scene of action I told the Wandorobo, small hunters clad only in spears and bows and arrows, that I was precious to the bwana and mustn't be killed. So one of them said I had better see whether I was capable of climbing a certain tree, before taking a shot.

Just as I was shinning up it, by way of a trial, up rode Bill, grey-faced with anger and very frightened. 'You don't know what a dangerous thing you're doing,' he exclaimed. I didn't dare tell him that the ammunition I had grabbed didn't fit the rifle, and the headman had had to return to the house to change it. However Bill, seeing everything in readiness, said I had better try and shoot the buffalo, and told me to aim for the eye. This I did, and no one was more surprised than I when it dropped like a stone. The rest of the herd took fright and galloped off. How pleased I was when a neighbour bought the skin. It enabled me to buy a much-needed iron bedstead and mattress, which I have to this day.

I don't know what we would have done without oxen. They did all the heavy work on the farm and took us to Nakuru on the rare occasions when we went there to buy groceries, which had to last about four months. We always tried to bring these back in packing-cases that we could use to make into furniture. The journey took several days there and back and we outspanned the oxen overnight. They were often scattered by lion during the hours of darkness and had to be gathered together in the morning before we could proceed. A pair of leaders cost £60, so we trained our own, first by yoking two together, then adding more pairs gradually and harnessing them to a tree-trunk.

For meat we depended on the gun: buck, buffalo, sometimes guinea-fowl, quail or sand-grouse. Bill always took a whistle with him when out shooting, to warn Africans not to rush up to the carcase when they heard a shot, but always to wait for the whistle. This precaution was the result of a fatal accident when a European had wounded a buffalo, and his gun-bearer, thinking to help his bwana, had approached from behind to finish it off. As he fired, the hunter stepped sideways and received the bullet himself.

The clothes we wore would seem strange nowadays: sun-helmets or double terais, of course, long boots, spine-pads made of red material. Our children were wrapped in leggings and woollen caps and never allowed out in the sun between 10 a.m. and 4 p.m. I remember the case of a sick child taken to be examined by a doctor in England and found to be suffering from rickets, due to lack of sunshine – in Kenya.

TEN

LONDIANI AND MAU SUMMIT

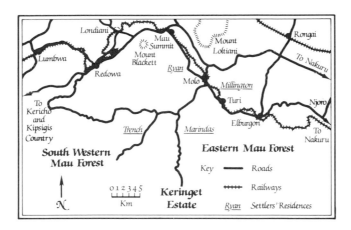

In 1903 the district was described by a traveller, Lord Hindlip, as 'about the coldest spot in East Africa'. As he had spent the night chasing escaped mules in the forest, he may have been jaundiced. The altitude of Mau Summit, the highest station on the line to Kisumu, is 8700 feet. So steep are the hills and so deep the ravines that 27 viaducts were needed to carry the line over the escarpment into the lake basin below.

In 1908 Mr A McGregor started the Forest Department's nursery which has populated many thousands of acres with young trees. After he retired he ran the Mount Blackett sawmill and later bought the Londiani Hotel. His great-grand-daughters are still living in Kenya.

Major Jack Drought, a colourful Irishman, bought large tracts of land before the First World War at sixpence an acre, and traded in cattle, hides and skins. In spite of a leg badly damaged in the first war he took part in the second, when the same leg was again wounded and he spent over a year in Mombasa Hospital. He lived to a ripe old age and is buried at Malindi.

E C Atkinson, brother of the Dr Atkinson who came to East Africa with Lord Delamere, lived on the farm known as Kampi Kongoni, and built many dams to encourage game and birds. The hotel, built by Lord Cranworth, was run by a third Atkinson brother and his wife before it was bought by Mr McGregor. It is now a thriving Harambee Secondary School. Will Evans and his brother Sam pioneered in mixed farming, and another pair of brothers, H S and R Smith, also weathered the storms of the thirties – locusts, drought and world depression – and their sons were still farming there in 1968.

Cara Buxton came out early in the century as a missionary, rode to Uganda on a mule and subsequently settled at Kedowa, where she virtually adopted the Kipsigis tribe wholesale and flatly refused to allow those in her employ to be punished for any misdemeanour, even when caught red-handed with stolen cattle. She was deeply imbued with East African history and its romance. 'She made me feel', wrote a neighbour, 'that I was Speke and Grant rolled into one and that with every step on the way from Londiani to the Mountains of the Moon I was walking through history.' Her nephew, Hubert Buxton, inherited her farm and his grand-daughters were living in Kericho in 1967 – four generations of the family.

Londiani used to be the railhead for Eldoret, 64 miles north west. Once off the train, the journey was a test of endurance on a track that rose 1500 feet through thick forest and, in places, ran through mud so appalling that whole teams of oxen were said to have vanished in it. One section was christened the Red Sea, and history records 28 days as the longest one-way trip – just over two miles a day. Return journeys averaged 30 days, until an enterprising Mr Whitelock started a passenger service with an American buckboard, and a change of bullocks every ten miles. After 1924, when the railway from Nakuru to Eldoret and beyond came into use, the importance of Londiani's station and hotel declined.

During the Second World War a large prisoner-of-war camp was set up in the district, and at one time 3000 Italian prisoners were living there. One of them, Dr Balletto, a companion of Felice Benuzzi in *No Picnic on Mount Kenya*, was the first medical officer of the cottage hospital. The camp site is now occupied by Forest Department offices and a mission. The Department has retained its connection with the district and still trains most of its forestry staff at the Londiani Training School.

Love on the Line

This letter, dated 1905, was addressed by the Londiani station master to his senior officer in Nairobi:
To the Traffic Manager,
Uganda Railway,
Nairobi.

Most Honoured and Respected Sir,

I have the honour to humbly and urgently require your Honour's permission to relieve me of my onerous duties at Londiani so as to enable me to visit the land of my nativity, to wit, India, forsooth.

This in order that I may take unto wife a damsel of many charms who has long been cherished in the heartbeats of my soul. She is of superfluous beauty and enamoured of the thought of becoming my wife. Said beauteous damsel has long been goal of my manly breast and now am fearful of other miscreant deposing me from her lofty affections. Delay in consummation may be ruination most damnable to romance of both damsel and your humble servant.

Therefore, I pray your Honour, allow me to hasten to India and contract marriage forthwith with said beauteous damsel. This being done happily I will return to Londiani to resume my fruitful official duties and perform also my maternal matrimonial functions. It is dead loneliness here without this charmer to solace my empty heart.

If your Honour will so far rejoice my soul to this extent and also as goes equally without saying that of said wife-to-be, I shall pray forever as in duty bound for your Honour's life-long prosperity, everlasting happiness, promotion of most startling rapidity and withal the fatherhood of many Godlike children to gambol playfully about your Honour's paternal knees to heart's content.

If, however, for reasons of State or other extreme urgency, the Presence cannot suitably comply with terms of this humble petition, then I pray your most excellent Superiority to grant me this benign favour for Jesus Christ's sake, a gentleman whom your Honour very much resembles.

I have the honour to be, Sir, your Honour's most humble and dutiful, but terribly love-sick, mortal withal.

(Signed)
B.A. (failed by God's misfortune) Bombay
Bombay University, and now Station Master, Londiani.

The request was granted.

Wildlife

by Marjorie Wilson

Before the turn of the century Londiani was unpopulated except for occasional nomads who came to hunt for meat and honey. Wildlife abounded. Elephant roamed on the forested slopes of Mount Loltiani, together with bongo and bushbuck. Vast herds of topi, Tommy and oribi ranged the grasslands together with buffalo and zebra, and the noble black-maned lion was far from rare.

Major Drought built a series of dams in order to water droves of cattle he was sending to market. Hyena and leopard took toll of these, and the Major paid a bounty to the herders on all predators they could destroy.

With the coming of the railway the first settlers arrived. They and their labour had to be fed. European farmers with rifles, and Africans with snares, maintained the meat supply, but with such a scant human population the numbers of the game did not decline.

Later the Forest Department, trying to reduce the ravages of bush and forest fires, cleared much indigenous timber and put in maize grown by families of African squatters, mainly Kikuyu. The Department followed this by starting forest plantations. The game inevitably destroyed much of the maize, and the early European farmers, trying to establish flax, maize and wheat, also had their

crops destroyed. The game was driven off by farmers and wardens, only to return in the breeding season to drop their young.

During the Second World War detachments of troops on their way north to the Western Desert camped at Londiani, and many a herd of topi and other game was turned into biltong. When the Italian prisoner-of-war camp was established, pelts

Almost every district built its church and club, and better buildings were put up as prosperity grew. The Church of St Andrew and St George at Londiani, a joint effort of Presbyterians and Anglicans, was completed in 1959. The Londiani Club had its cricket ground laid out to the measurements of the Kennington Oval

and skins were exchanged for cigarettes and other commodities, by the prisoners. Buck were regularly shot to feed the camp. After the war came more farmers, cultivation was intensified, and no game could be tolerated near the valuable wheat shambas.

Gradually the hyena disappeared, together with the leopard, now officially listed in the Red Data Book as on the way to extinction. Only a few bushbuck, reedbuck, oribi and dik-dik survived on the farms.

The vervet monkey still comes out of the forest every year as the maize is ripening and does considerable damage. The colobus also appears occasionally, bounding from tree to tree, but being a leaf-eater does not damage the crops.

Now all one sees on a moonlight night, or in the headlamps of a car, is an occasional jackal, hare or antbear. The few remaining buck and small herds of buffalo have retreated into what survives of the dense forest, and that, too, is shrinking rapidly.

Wool-dyeing at home

by Audrey Clarke

For those of us who keep sheep in this district and are lucky enough to have a spinning-wheel it is a delight to be able to spin our wool and dye it in a variety of shades from the many indigenous plants available.

Rubia (*gakaraku* to the Kikuyu) climbs over every hedgerow and its roots yield a very pleasing reddish dye. *Magatio* (again a Kikuyu name), which looks rather like an elongated dock, gives a deep and fast yellow dye from its roots. (Incidentally these roots are much prized for their medicinal value.) The senecio, with massed heads of bright yellow flowers, gives a delightful soft yellow if the flowers are used when they have just come out. Then that splendid little bush of the indigo family gives a clear blue if mordanted with sulphuric acid, or a lovely warm brown, which is fast, if steeped for three days and simmered with the wool.

All these plants give their dye best if they are soaked for at least 24 hours before the wool is added to the water and the mixture heated. The roots should first be cleaned of earth and then scraped in the dye bath, as the dye is in a thin skin which covers the root. For a deep colour add more roots. Both the leaves and the stems of the indigo steeped together give a dye. In every case the dye bath should simmer, but not boil. Forty minutes should be sufficient, but sometimes it is possible to see the wool has absorbed all the colour in a shorter time, leaving the water clear.

Leave the wool to cool in the dye bath and then rinse several times in cold water and hang up to dry.

One warning: sufficient wool for the purpose required should be dyed at one time as, with vegetable dyes, it is not easy to repeat the exact shade.

All these plants will give pleasing shades and keep their colour. Be sure that the wool has been spun at an even tension, as if there is much variation in the twist the wool won't take the dye evenly.

ELEVEN

MOLO AND TURI

Molo Road

The Molo downs are bleak and beautiful. They rise to an altitude of 9000 feet and a cold wind sweeps over them. In the distance is the dark line of the Mau forest, but most of the plateau is grassland with scattered clumps of trees. It was too cold for the Maasai on one side and the Kipsigis on the other, and so was uninhabited when the railway survey parties arrived.

The line came in 1900 and the first settlers soon after. One of the earliest was E Powys Cobb who, in about 1905, took up a wide stretch of land called Keringet. These rolling open downlands seemed made for wheat. But ploughing with teams of oxen and a single-furrow plough scarcely scratched the surface, and oxen fared badly in the cold. Tractors lay in the future. However, steam engines were in fashion. Powys Cobb imported two, and placed one at each end of the furrow. With a chain and winch, the engines hauled a plough to and fro between them. Powys Cobb also imported reapers-and-binders, and a threshing machine.

Molo looked inviting to cereals but it was not. The story of wheat growing in the Kenya highlands is one of an unremitting, and still continuing, battle against many strains of rust. Powys Cobb had little success until the variety named Equator was bred in about 1910 by Lord Delamere at his Equator Ranch at Njoro.

In 1908 Jasper Abraham imported Romney rams to improve the cross already made in the Rift Valley between local Maasai ewes and imported Merino rams. Later, his son imported Corriedales.

One of the major scourges of the East African highlands, for which no remedy

Gertrude Hill-Williams joined her husband on Morindas in 1908, bringing out her two small daughters, and Miss Bull to look after them. This picture, taken by Mr Hill-Williams at Keringet in 1910 shows Emily Bull (later Mrs Cross) holding Neddy, and Kathleen (Twopence) and Hilda Hill-Williams with Dick Gethin, who then worked for Powys-Cobb, between them. Note the 'true' Dorobo dog now prized in the UK and called Basenji. Widowed in 1917 Mrs Hill-Williams continued farming at Molo and later at Mweiga until 1930, when she built the Sportsman's Arms at Nanyuki.

was then known, was horse-sickness. Molo was free of it, and horse-breeding was soon established. In 1910 Powys Cobb imported an Arab stallion, Talisman, who became a famous sire. Among his progeny were several outstanding winners (Tamash, Tally-Ho) and he got his last foal, Talc, a notable winner belonging to D H Pell-Smith, when he was 34 years old.

After the Second World War the European Settlement Board came into being, and by 1949 had bought and split up two Molo farms, those of S H Mews and Eric Crake, each farm measuring 7000 acres. Later a third farm of 9000 acres was bought and divided for closer settlement. Heavy machinery now made possible the building of large dams, enabling the plateau to support twice as many livestock.

The Government opened a Pasture Research Station and the poor indigenous grasses were replaced by cocksfoot, ryegrass and subterranean and Louisiana white clovers. The carrying capacity of the district rose from one beast per six acres in 1907 to one per two acres in 1967. The barren plateau of 1907 had become, by 1967, a prosperous farming area, paddocked, watered, treed and fenced, and carrying some of the best livestock in the country.

The Church on the Hill

by the Rev. P Price

The first organized church services were held in the dak bungalow on Molo Station in 1921. Most of the congregation came on horseback. The arrival of an occasional 'mixed' train, with goods and passenger coaches, was a major disadvantage. The hissing of steam, and the full-throated noise of passengers and onlookers gathered on the platform, were not conducive to the spirit of worship, so another venue was sought.

This was found a few years later at the Cross Roads Inn, where a larger, quieter and altogether more suitable room was lent by the proprietor, Mr Cross. It was, however, not a church, so an appeal was launched for funds to build one. E N Millington and the Abraham brothers were leading spirits, and land was given by the Government.

Only local materials were used in the construction of St Alban's – old cedar for all external timbers, and olive (*msharagi*) for the heavy roof timbers. Hand-made bricks for filling between timber studs added to the mellowness. There were no nails. It was a labour of love.

The Molo Hunt

(i) Landmarks *by David Furse*

The Molo Hunt started in 1922, with hounds from the Masara Hunt, which came to an end in that year. Hunting existed at Molo, however, many years earlier. Powys Cobb's hounds hunted the district for some seasons before and during the First World War. This pack consisted of half-bred bloodhounds, and their huntsman was Gerry Alexander, who was Master and Huntsman of the Molo Hunt from its start until 1944.

At the end of the First World War some hounds still remained in Mr Cobb's kennels at Keringet. A pride of lions started cattle-killing on the southern boundary of the estate, which adjoined Maasai country. The pack hunted and bayed up six lions, all of which were destroyed. This was their last hunt.

In 1924 the Molo (foxhound) pack was enlarged by taking over the Lumbwa hounds. One of the chief difficulties was appallingly high mortality among puppies. Tick-fever is particularly virulent in the district, and in some seasons not a single puppy was reared. Puppies were sent out to other districts to walk, which was successful.

In 1936 Walter Trench returned from a holiday in Ireland with a stallion hound, Hermit, and two brood bitches from the Scarteen Hunt. Walter Trench and Jim Ryan built kennels at the former's farm and started to breed the 'Black-and-Tans'. New drafts from the Fernie and other English packs were added. In 1944 George Danby hunted the hounds for three years and then Jim Ryan took over. With him was Kariuki Gichero, who came in 1947 as Kennel Huntsman after ten years' previous experience with packs at Mweiga, Kipkabus, Sotik and

Naro Moru. Mr C D Cullen, Master of the Copston Hunt at Kipkabus, wrote of him: 'He has a devotion to the job, an eye for the country and a cast-iron nerve. No day is too long for him and he is a fearless horseman.' He completed 30 years as a Hunt Servant and then retired. In 1965 Jim Ryan handed over to his son Pip, the last Master.

The hounds usually hunted reedbuck, and occasionally jackal. No other quarry was permissible.

(ii) The last hunt *by Jack Ensoll*

We met at Marindas, 9000 feet up on the old Barnett place, and I remembered how John Barnett had complained as reedbuck played hide-and-seek around a few acres below a copse, 'Always the same, this time of year, out of one wheat-field and into another.' Then the wheat was beginning to stand high and was the signal for the end of another Molo season. Now it was just a slight green bloom on the brown land under a leaden sky, and I leaned from the saddle and picked everlasting flowers as we moved off to draw.

Kariuki put hounds into covert beside a stream and before long we heard the brassy summons of the Gone Away, the music of a good pack running, the rumble of fast cantering horses and the crack as they took their fences. Our pilot took us straight uphill, up one of those labouring, high-altitude hills, and we checked in the woodland at the top. Now and then the panting and rustle of a hound at work, and again a burst of music as they broke covert, and we were away down the far side of Marindas and running fast towards Summerhills, and all that magnificent, galloping Molo country was at our feet.

The sweet African wind whistled past our ears and the damp earth flew from the hooves of the horses ahead, and the astounded sheep drew together and watched. Through a swamp and over a fence in the wire and at the far side of Summerhills I gave it best and watched them go, the hounds a swift-moving pattern of black, white and tan, Kariuki and the whips diminutive galloping figures in red, and the rest of the field behind.

Some of the flowers which grow in the Uasin Gishu.

TWELVE

ELDORET AND ITS NEIGHBOURHOOD

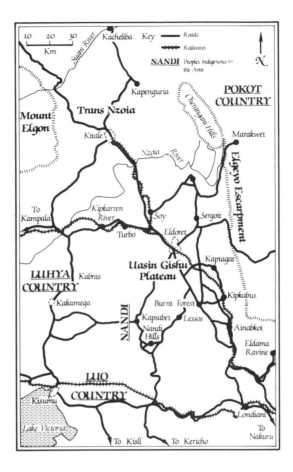

The Uasin Gishu Plateau lies to the west of the Rift Valley, sloping gently from 8000 feet in the south east near Kipkabus to 6000 feet at Turbo in the north west.

At many places in the district can be seen 'Sirikwa holes'. They are relics of a people whose settlements consisted of round excavated dwellings with stone walls. This people withdrew to Mount Elgon, probably early in the nineteenth century after a crushing defeat by the Maasai, and finally disappeared.

A branch of the Maasai replaced them for a while. But in time they themselves were routed by another section of Maasai and moved away to the south. The rolling open grasslands of the plateau, bounded by forested escarpments, were left to the wild game.

The ultimate doom of these millions of animals was sealed on that day, early in 1901, when the first white man with a rifle climbed up the escarpment from Eldama Ravine.

From a Letter Addressed to Mr A Cloete:

27 July 1955

Dear Anaak,

Yes, this long ago history you will have to show John de Waal, as he knows a lot about the things that happened then.

Bon van Breda was pushed over the Portuguese Boundary by the English Forces in 1900 with other Burghers, as also John de Waal, but Bon managed to get away from the army and by slow stages arrived in Lourenço Marques. From there in early 1901 he took ship to Dar es Salaam and Mombasa. He worked sub-contracting somewhere near Nakuru. From there he joined a small party on a shooting expedition. They passed Eldama Ravine and on to the Plateau by native footpaths in 1901. In 1902, at the termination of the S.A. war, he went back and brought his two brothers, Dirk and Piet, with him in the middle of 1903. They applied and each received 10 000 acres.

At the end of 1903 Dirk met Dad in Jo'burg and told him about the country. At the end of 1904 Dad and I came up, but the war with the Nandi was on. I stayed in Naivasha . . . .

. . . In October 1905 my Father and family arrived, also John de Waal in 1906 approx. One month after, Janie and Jan Viljoen came with their families. Together we trekked up to Nakuru with our stock, with untrained oxen . . . .

. . . At the beginning of 1907 Dad and John de Waal and D and B van Breda took a trolley on the Sclater's Road, and that was the first wagon ever to be on the Plateau. Shortly after that I took our big wagon with Mother, Madge and Jos through. This was a very hard journey. So our family was the first to be on the Plateau as a family . . . .

. . . At the end of 1908 van Rensburg's trek came in. They all landed at Nakuru. After an expedition to the Plateau, they left early in 1909 (March approx.) I went with them, taking a load for us. From 1907, the first time we went up with the family, there was always one or other of us on the Plateau with the sheep and cattle . . . .

Ever yours,

C V Cloete
(C Valerius 'Sonnie' Cloete)

Recollections of Cecil Hoey

(written in 1956)

It was in about 1905 that I met at Naivasha a very nice Afrikaner by the name of Van Breda who was keen on taking up land. Having heard of the wonderful shooting on the Uasin Gishu I made a safari . . . It would be almost impossible to describe the vast quantities of game I encountered. Jackson's hartebeest roamed over the country in herds three to five hundred strong, eland in herds of 200 or

Transporting wheat to railhead

more, and zebra literally by the thousand, to say nothing of numerous lions and some very fine elephants which used to travel between the Elgeyo Forest and Mount Elgon.

I made my standing camp at Lake Sergoit, and often I would spend the day on Sergoit Rock with my glasses, watching the vast herds of game below me. It was on one of these occasions that I turned my glasses in the direction of the Burnt Forest and there I saw a white streak in the forest. At first it looked like a river, then I thought it might be smoke, but it gradually became too defined in shape, and eventually, after some hours, I could see it was moving. It turned out to be the first Afrikaner Trek to the Plateau. These were all the tents of the wagons following one another on a track, which was being cut to make the first road.

The next day I went and met the big trek, and there I found a grand old man, Jansen Van Rensburg, and many other splendid fellows who have since passed away, who were the first ones to open up the country and to prove that a living could be made off the land. A fine man was Arnoldi, who afterwards in the First World War formed Arnoldi's Scouts and did wonderful war service and who, I believe, was killed in action . . .

Soon after, settlement moved ahead, and many of us engaged Nandi squatters. The warriors were fine fellows with the most indomitable courage, and we had many lion-hunts when the Nandi would surround a lion and gradually close in and completely encircle it, a wonderful sight in all their war paint. Invariably the lion charged and a Nandi moran (up till then they were in a crouching position with shields held ahead and spears poised to strike) would rise to his full height, let out a war-cry and take the lion on his shield, thrusting hard with his spear. In a fraction of a second the other warriors closed and riddled the lion with spear thrusts. Then came the triumphant song of victory as each warrior, shoulder to

FARMS 121/2
P. O. ELDORE RIVER.

Uasin Gish
British

Standard, P. & P. Works.

M̶r̶. Messrs C & A Cripps

Dr. to NOLLOSEGELLA

Sept 1911
1 To Cash
   Cigs 2 5/12 lds Wimbi 4/60 /25 2/50
   By Undercharge on sheep 2 Tea
   4 pkts Cigs 4/42 6¼ lds Wimbi 11/88
5 10 By Sheep & Goat skins /50 1 lgtt rod iron 1/30
12 Beads & soap M'Bruki /50
    ½ doz wicks /50
20 2 2/3 lds Wimbi 6/97 Painkiller 1/50

Oct 4 100 lbs Wimbi
5 1 Sunlight Soap

                         85'   43.47
                         79.81   42 09
                                    84.56
                         cr 5.19

9. XI. XI.   By cheque with thanks
                  SOC___ STORE
                  H.O.L.

No Stamps to be had at
Township   Net Cash.

E. & O. E.

shoulder and twirling their spears in the air, danced round the dead lion chanting their war songs. Nearly every good kill was accompanied by a warrior being mauled by the lion and never did we go on a lion hunt without medical aid such as bandages and disinfectants . . .

After I started farming, I grew a very good maize crop; the question then was how to get sufficient labour to harvest it. As I had shot a good many elephant to the benefit of the Cherangani Wandorobo who feasted on the meat, I thought I would enlist them to come and help with the harvest. They responded immediately and came down in large numbers to work – on condition I shot them ten *kongoni* to eat before they started. After two or three days to recover from their feast, we started on the harvest, which went splendidly. When it was over I produced a bag of rupees and offered to pay them. They looked at the rupees, and said, 'What's the use of these things?' I tried to explain they could buy soap and sugar, but they refused to have anything to do with the rupees. I then asked what they would like as a reward, and they said, 'Give us each a box of matches.' These they carefully tied up in little bits of skin, as the only means of making fire they had was by rubbing two sticks together. Then, having had a further feast of meat, they returned happily to their homes.

Sixty-four

When Government surveyors pegged out blocks of land for which settlers could apply, each future farm received a number. Number 64, on the Sosiani River, was leased to Willie van Aardt. He found it unsuitable for farming, so it was selected as the site of a Post Office, opened in 1910. Telegrams went by heliograph to Kapsabet, the nearest point where there was a telegraph line. This township in embryo was known as '64' until officially named Eldoret in 1912 by the Governor. By then the European population of the Plateau had grown to 153 males, 96 females and 236 children, half of these under ten.

Some Plateau Personalities

J McNab Mundell

. . . arrived at the place where Eldoret now stands in 1910. His uncle, John, was Chief of the Clan McNab and the Mundells claim direct descent from Robert the Bruce. He opened a little trading store with Wreford Smith which soon afterwards acquired the dignity and importance of becoming the local post office. To this was added a bar, the 'Ratpit', which had its door broken about 3 a.m. one night by a very thirsty person. The door was not replaced for a whole year and during that time the few settlers in the vicinity helped themselves to the stock when they pleased and left in payment either cash or chits. It is interesting to note that not a cent was lost.

J C Shaw

. . . came to open a branch of the Standard Bank of South Africa in a room adjoining Eddie's Bar (the Ratpit). When the safe was off-loaded from the wagon it fell against the mud wall and knocked over the bank. The bank was then rebuilt round the safe. It had a counter, and Mr Shaw used to take his morning bath behind it before starting business, after a preliminary visit in his dressing-gown and slippers to Eddie's Bar.

The first bank in Eldoret was this mud-walled, tin-roofed structure erected in 1912 for the Standard Bank of South Africa. On the left is the original manager, Mr J C Shaw, with his wife and an onlooker. The building continued on the left (not shown in photograph) into Eddie's Bar and early citizens of the township used the bank for cashing cheques and the bar next door for spending their money

H C Kirk

... trekked up here in 1907 and ran the Sergoit Store for A C Hoey. He married Amy in the District Commissioner's office. The DC N E F Corbett, did not like marrying people, so he went on safari and they were married by J C Shaw. A quarter of the way through the service he decided it was enough. There was no marriage register in those days. Twenty-two years later friends were surprised to see an announcement of their marriage; their son, Rex, had gone to America to learn under Massey Harris and had been asked for the marriage certificate of his parents. Rex was later Mayor of Eldoret.

Mrs John de Waal

. . . , then Mrs Dreyer, arrived on 31 January 1911 and travelled all over the countryside as a District Nurse on a mule, in all weathers. There was only one doctor, Dr Heard, who also went everywhere on a mule, and it was said that no call was ever refused. Mrs Dreyer delivered nine of Mrs A Cloete's 13 children. She was the first to have light from the power station (built in 1933) in her nursing home.

Juma Hajee

... a Muslim with 3 sons and 6 daughters, came to Kenya in 1904 from India. In 1907 he came up to the Plateau and lived 11 miles from Eldoret at what is still called Hajee's Drift, where he had a store on van Breda's land. Later he also had shops at Kakamega, Sergoit, Karuna, Marakwet and Eldama Ravine. There was no bridge over the river at Farm 64 then, only one fallen tree, and to cross the river people went as far as Hajee's Drift. Mr Hajee served on the Eldoret Municipal Council for ten years.

J van Rensburg

... brought up the first large trek in the 'Windhoek'. Those pioneers consisted of

47 families including two Predikants. From Mombasa they arrived at Nakuru in five special trains on 18 June 1908. They brought with them 42 wagons and 72 horses and from Nakuru they travelled in two columns and blazed the wagon trail to their new home.

Abraham Joubert

. . . owned Farm No. 1 on the plateau. He lived to be 97, and at 90 still made his own shoes.

L. A. Johnson

. . . an American, was celebrated for his hospitality. One day Mr Mayer, proprietor and editor of the *East African Standard*, arrived and was invited for the night. At breakfast the next morning he said to LA, 'Do you get your East African Weekly regularly?' LA said, 'Sometimes it don't hap up.' He was asked what he did then, and replied, 'We just use grass.' In 1930 LA discovered gold at Kakamega and started the first farmers' syndicate. A few months later there were over 1000 prospectors.

Mr Barker

. . . used to ride round and tell everyone the news. He was much put out when wireless came in and there was no news to tell. He died through taking a three months' supply of sleeping pills in one dose.

Mrs Ortlepp

. . . was a widow who had her face lifted several times and had permanent pink on her cheeks. She had married wealthy Mr Ortlepp, a surveyor from South Africa who built a township which he called Ortleppville (now part of Eldoret). When he died in 1932 he was buried in Eldoret, but Mrs Ortlepp wished him to be re-buried in South Africa. She asked the DC whether, in view of the high cost of transporting coffins, she could put the remains in a box marked 'Bones'. The answer was no, so Mr Ortlepp remained where he was. Mrs Ortlepp kept a tame cheetah, and at 60 years old won a competition for the best lady's legs.

E L Steyn Snr

. . . worked as hard as any, ploughing with a team of 16 oxen, broadcasting the seed himself by hand from an old buckskin apron, and reaping wheat with a sickle. Then came the visiting threshing machine which would thresh 50 to 100 bags at a time. He would buy this amount from the farmer there and then – no middlemen, forms, restrictions, regulations or red tape to reduce profits.

Lt-Col G A Swinton-Home

. . . took up land at Soy after coming from India on a shooting safari before the First World War. By 1914 his place at Soy had become quite a village with his flour and posho mills, stores and hotel. He served with distinction in the First World War, gaining a DSO, and returned to develop cattle and sheep rearing, maize, coffee and other crops, and to be at the forefront of every enterprise in the Soy area. He died in 1960, in his 85th year.

A Lessos Wedding

by Mrs Eileen Williams

In 1911 my dad (Mr Leslie) came here to Lessos and bought two farms, so in 1912 he chartered a small German vessel to bring up some of his stock from South Africa: 100 merino sheep: 20 purebred cows and a bull; 17 horses; 7 dogs; 10 young chickens; 2 kittens; his 2 daughters and a nephew; and his wife. Also 2 young men to help feed and water the stock on the boat daily. The two young men were too seasick to help, and the heavy work fell on my dad and his nephew. He also brought two wagons, two traps and harness, saddlery, etc.

My sister became engaged the very evening our boat left Durban, she was then only 18. In December 1913 she was married to Bennet Mousley in Eldoret. Our little bamboo church was specially built for the occasion. Our kind neighbours inspanned their oxen and trekked to the 'whipstick bush' about 30 or 40 miles to cut and carry the bamboos and load them on to their wagons. They also had to bring cedar posts for the uprights, and then the church was thatched with grass which was cut by them. In those early days there were no Africans living on the Plateau, so it was all done by our very kind neighbours and friends.

The great day came, after days of cooking by my mother for a reception of over 100 guests, and also a dance. It took us a whole day to trek the 20 miles to Eldoret. The reception was held at the school kindly lent to our parents.

Londiani was our shopping centre then. We got in a six months' supply of provisions at one time, as it often took the transport riders up to a month to travel those 60 miles there and back, and a terrible time they used to have.

In those early days there were no servants and we used to carry water up from the spring about 200 yards below our house for washing and cooking – and what a lot of clothes we had to wash. There were five lots of men's khaki clothes as well as our own.

Two delightful old bachelors used to walk ten miles every Sunday bringing us a week's supply of vegetables and fruit. All told, it was a happy life.

Growing up in Eldoret

by Mrs Dorothy Hughes, MBE, FRIBA

I arrived in Eldoret on my third birthday, having travelled by ox-wagon from Londiani with my parents, Mr and Mrs Max Ullmann. Once it took us three weeks to do the 60 miles from Londiani owing to the mud; sometimes things got so bad that the drivers would have to light fires under the noses of the oxen to get them to rise.

When we arrived Eldoret had only one building, of mud and wattle, which was the bank, post office and rest-house combined. My father built the first shop of wood and iron in the main street for J H S Todd, and they stocked everything needed for farmers. It had a lovely wide verandah back and front, and I always said this building was the start of my interest in architecture.

Top: the first church wedding:
Bennet Mousley to Miss Leslie

Middle: Dorothy Ullmann on a
Holt tractor

Bottom: Eldoret in the early
1920s

The DC, Mr Schofield, had regular parties for the few children in Eldoret. He would put a large bottle of castor oil on the table and tell the children they could eat as much as they liked but they'd have to take a dose afterwards. I went to a little school run by Mr and Mrs Humphries when I was four years old. We were in Eldoret during the Nandi rising when many homesteads were burnt down and the women and children were put into a laager for safety.

Later my father worked for Gailey and Roberts, and at one of the early Shows in Eldoret he got me to drive one of their tractors, doing figures-of-eight, with a notice on the side of the tractor reading 'Even a child can control the Holt'. We sold many tractors at the Show in opposition to my future husband John, who was then with T J O'Shea selling Fordsons, and I always said that he married me in order to beat the competition.

A New Order

Today the Uasin Gishu is a thriving land of arable fields, paddocks, dams and plantations which exports grain, meat and other produce to the rest of Kenya and the world beyond. Eldoret is a growing town with a number of modern industries. The Municipal Board created in 1929 has given way to an elected Council with a Mayor, a coat of arms, a mace and all the trimmings. The first African Mayor, Alderman Alex Oloo, took office in 1963. Most of the Afrikaners have trekked away, this time in cars and lorries, and most of the British farmers have gone too. Their lands and houses have been taken over by African farmers who are carrying on what they began. The wild animals belong to the past.

These items are from the East African Standard:

(i) 22 March 1968 More than 60 of the world's finest Boran cattle were railed to Uganda this week, an event which marked the end of a famous farming story in Kenya. The cattle – 37 bulls and 28 cross-bred heifers, and cows with calves at foot – were the final consignment sold by the former Kakeptui Stud farm, near Turbo, which was owned by Mr Derek Haggie.

The animals, the last of 13 generations bred by Mr Haggie and his wife Hilda, were bought by Uganda Livestock Industries, Kampala, a state-controlled organization now in the throes of setting up a beef complex which will eventually rival the Kenya Meat Commission.

The consignment of bulls, whose maximum age is 3 years and 3 months, was the biggest known single quota of quality Boran males to leave Kenya.

Top: a fine Boran bull from Kakeptui

Bottom: Mr Derek Haggie

(ii) 4 March 1968 President Kenyatta's attendance at the Eldoret Show boosted the crowd to record proportions. Entries were high and African farmers did very well in the livestock section.

The championship event was highlighted when Mr Samuel Simam lifted the Supreme Title with his Jersey bull, Highfield Proud Rebel. Cattle judges highly commended the condition of the bull and the way it had been prepared for display. The chief cattle steward said Mr Simam had opened the way for more African farmers to win big prizes at national agricultural shows.

THIRTEEN
TRANS NZOIA

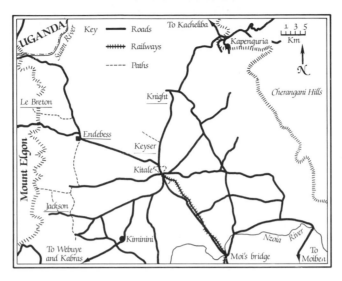

The Trans Nzoia is an area of some 1150 square miles lying in the north-western corner of Kenya. In the west it is dominated by Mount Elgon, so called from the Ol Konye, an offshoot of the Maasai who once inhabited the upper slopes. Its highest peak in Kenya – it lies partly in Uganda – is Wagagai, 14 178 feet. In its forest, elephant, buffalo and leopard were once common; birds, butterflies and wild flowers still abound; there are good trout streams and exciting caves.

To the east lie the Cherangani Hills with even more varied scenery, the habitat of the rare *bongo* and a nesting-place for Lammergeyers. Between these two mountains, at an altitude of 6000 to 8000 feet, is to be found some of the best agricultural land in Kenya. The River Nzoia divides the district from the Uasin Gishu.

Kitale (spelt Quitale on old maps), almost in the middle, is 250 miles from Nairobi, and lies on one of the old slave routes from Uganda to the coast. In the car park of the club there is a circle of stones which is said to have had a ring in the centre to which slaves were fastened during the night.

From the Recollections of Abu Bakr

I, Abu Bakr, was born in British Somaliland, but when I was a boy of about 14 I crossed to Aden and was there taken into service as personal servant to Captain Maddicks of the Uganda Rifles, who was recruiting there. I went with him to Mombasa, where he was training the *askaris* that he had recruited. This was in 1897. We then entrained on the newly-built railway and it took us four days, with many derailments, to reach Voi. We went on for one further day by rail to Tsavo, which was railhead.

From there we formed a caravan of porters and marched for ten days to Kibwezi in the Ukamba country, where we halted for about a fortnight. From Kibwezi it was a safari of 14 days to Machakos, and from there a five-day safari to the Nairobi River. We camped to the west of the river about where the original race-course was made later. There were, of course, no Europeans or town there then, but there were Maasai on the hill where Nairobi Club and State House now stand. There were no Kikuyu then, only Maasai, who brought us many head of cattle which were slaughtered for our company.

We camped by the Nairobi River for a couple of days and then went on one day further to the home of Mr Hall at Kabete; it was here that we first met the Kikuyu. From there a two-day safari brought us to the Escarpment, which we descended by a track that had been cut for Captain Lugard by Mr Dick and Major Sclater. We then marched for four or five days to Naivasha; the askaris were very heavily laden as most of the porters that we had engaged had run away.

At Naivasha there was a large *boma* with Mr Wilson as DC. The lake reached almost to the *boma* and the Morendat beyond Naivasha was in flood. We camped here for about three weeks while the troops were ferried across . . . There were Maasai as far as Lake Elmenteita but not beyond, as they did not like the grazing around Nakuru. We did not stay long at Nakuru, where there was only the lake and no inhabitants, but continued our safari for another seven days via Kampi ya Moto to Eldama Ravine. The main body of our troops was now close at hand, pursuing the Nubian mutineers who were at Baringo; we joined up and followed the mutineers as they retreated into Uganda.

Abu Bakr then marched with his company of the Uganda Rifles over the escarpment to Kabras, where: 'the Nandi were frightened of the Kabras and the Kabras were frightened of the Nandi; the Maasai seemed to be the only tribe that were not frightened of their neighbours.' After a pause at Chief Mumia's, who 'made his people help us in every way', they marched on into Busoga in Uganda and took part in quelling the Sudanese mutiny between 1897 and 1899. In 1900 he was engaged as personal servant to Sir Harry Johnstone, Special Commissioner for Uganda. On his way back to the coast early in 1900 Johnstone, accompanied by Geoffrey Archer, reached the still unexplored western slopes of Mount Elgon. 'Sir Harry had a book to which he frequently referred,' Abu Bakr commented, 'and was in search of a reported land which was cool and empty of inhabitants.' They camped at Kacheliba, and then marched south to the bottom of a range of hills lying across their path. Abu Bakr continues:
A report came in that some elephants had been seen near the top of the hills, so Mr Archer and some others and I climbed the hill to shoot the elephants. These went on up and over the brow and we found that the range of hills was an escarpment leading up to an immense plain, which we now know as Trans Nzoia. There were no trees on the plain, but long grass which, under the influence of the wind went rippling away into the distance like the sea.

I immediately returned to camp and told Sir Harry what I had seen; he came back with me, and with his book climbed up with me to see the land that he had been looking for. (This took place on what is now Padre Knight's farm.)

On the next day the whole safari climbed the escarpment and proceeded in a south-easterly direction, across a flooded stream on what was later Major Keyser's farm. We went on to the site of Kitale and camped near the present site of the Mohammedan School. On the way from Moroto we had not seen a single African, it was all uninhabited country.

We stayed in this camp for about ten days while Sir Harry wrote in his book. There were no trees at all and we had to use the droppings of elephants, buffalo, zebra, eland, etc. as fuel for our fires, as they abounded on these plains.

We then continued towards the south and on the second day we reached the Nzoia River where we camped. When our porters went down to the river they saw human footprints in the mud; they called out to us, and we followed the tracks until we lost them. Captain Wilson of the KAR looked up into the trees lining the river, the first trees that we had seen on these plains, and reported some large birds in the higher branches. The porters saw that they were men cowering in the branches, as high as they could get.

We ordered them to come down, which they eventually did, and we took them to Sir Harry Johnstone for questioning. There was a woman in our safari who knew both Swahili and Maasai and she interpreted.

The three men said they were Wandorobo from the Cherangani; they told him that the river was the Nzoia and the other stream flowing in at that point was the Moiben. They said that although now the land was almost uninhabited – there were only 29 of their clan left – yet formerly it had been fully inhabited by Maasai who had died or left the district. Some had died of illness, others had been killed in wars with the Suk (now Pokot), and the remainder had mostly gone off in the direction of Ravine. This had happened before they were born.

We stayed on the Nzoia for five days, while Sir Harry wrote down all that he had been told. The three men then came on with us as our guides; after another four days of safari we came to a large expanse of water, about two miles across but only a couple of feet deep. It stretched across and away so we waded through it and camped here for six days, and Sir Harry had a survey beacon put up on Sergoit hill. The lake there is now very much smaller. Except for the three Wandorobo men on the Nzoia, we saw no inhabitants in any of the country until we got to Eldama Ravine. From Ravine we went to Mau Summit, which was then the end of the railway. This was in August 1901.

The Elgon Caves

by Renshaw Mitford Barberton

When we came up to the Trans Nzoia to settle, early in 1913, one of the first adventures we had was to visit two large caves in the foothills of Mount Elgon. There were several Maasai families living in these caves with all their cattle, sheep and goats, safely stockaded off in the deeper and darker passages, some of which extended over 150 yards into the cliffs.

These caves appeared mostly to be man-made as wherever one looked there were thousands of axe or chisel marks on the walls. The inhabitants told us that the rock contained salt and that it was always being dug up and pounded for their animals. We discovered no less than 38 caves of which about six were occupied by Maasai and their stock. In later years, when the district became more settled, the Government made all the cave-dwelling people move out and build on the hills where conditions were more hygienic, and where they could be counted for tax.

Many of these caves were also occupied by millions of bats and we were able to procure many tons of bat guano, which we sold to coffee farmers as fertilizer.

All the lower foothills of Mount Elgon are pierced by caves, and over the years we explored over 50 miles of cliffs in our cave-hunting safaris. In one big volcanic cave on Farm No. 7, which we christened Hampton Court, we laid binder twine along the major passages, and there must be about four or five miles of twine there now.

The highest cave on Elgon is about 13 000 feet and this is entirely man-made. Here the workers have followed a thin stratum of soda or phosphate. There are many passages, all interconnected, and in no place is the roof more than three feet above the floor. This cave was still being worked by the stock-owning Africans who then lived above the forest on the mountain.

The explorer, Joseph Thomson, the first European to visit Mount Elgon in 1885, was convinced that the caves he saw were man-made. This I think is correct in the case of many of the smaller caverns, but the huge caves which cover many miles of tunnels and acres in area, although extensively chipped, must have had a volcanic origin.

Soldier Settlers, 1920

by Marjorie Pharazyn

How we ever found our farm was a miracle – only a compass to guide us, plus one or two vintage settlers who resented our intrusion into their own happy hunting ground and gave us misleading directions.* We arrived one evening on the banks of the Nzoia River, having trekked from Londiani with a wagon, Scotch cart and 32 oxen, our drivers, servants, stores and tents, a few hens, four cows, and a grey parrot who perched on top of the lot and whose cry 'Come on! Come on!' encouraged our progress.

We had to dig a ford to get our wagons across. Then we had to locate our land, which we had selected from a blueprint in the East African office in London. Iron beacons about three feet high were not easy to spot in tall grass twice that height.

The first auction sale of land in the Trans Nzoia took place on 24 March 1913 in Nairobi, when 22 leases found purchasers; nearly one third of the lots were withdrawn unsold.

Trees grew thickly on the lower slopes of the Cherangani Hills, so clearing land and digging out tree-stumps had to be started without delay. Our kitchen was a grass shelter and our oven a hollowed-out ant-hill which produced excellent bread and roast joints. We lived entirely by our guns, and on some groceries brought out from England.

Some of our men had brought their families, and the children were set to work rolling wet clay into balls the size of ostrich eggs. When set in rows in the sun these became very hard, and then the women built them into walls for our first houses. These walls became hard as pisé, but did not join up to the roof, leaving a wide gap between wall and roof. Nights could be cold, and we burned charcoal in perforated *debes*.

Kitale did not exist. Eldoret was 44 miles away, and the nearest railhead at Londiani 100 miles, where we had to send all our maize by ox-wagon. This was a three-week safari, and farm work suffered by the absence of a team for that period. We rode mules for personal transport. One of our first undertakings was to build a bridge over the Nzoia at the bottom of the farm, strong enough to carry our wagons loaded with maize; the marvel is that they never fell over the edges which were quite unprotected. A trip to Nairobi was a major enterprise. By mule-cart to Eldoret, then by trotting ox-cart service we travelled through the dark night, stopping every ten miles to change oxen and drivers, to Londiani, where we transferred to the Uganda Railway. The old-fashioned carriages were roomy and one took one's own bedding if one wanted any. When the train stopped at meal-times all the passengers got out for delightful meals served in the station dining room of fresh eggs, tea, bread and butter and jam, and much chat with one's fellow travellers.

The arrival of the railway at Eldoret in 1924 simplified many problems. The day the first train arrived was a gala one; the engine, decorated with flags, flowers, and bundles of wheat, bore the Governor, Sir Robert Coryndon, to the sound of cheering crowds. When it reached Kitale the following year, the wild and woolly days of the Trans Nzoia came to an end. Soon there were schools, banks, hospitals, churches, town plans, Boards, a branch of the EAWL, committees, political meetings, and 'civilization' had arrived.

Life on the Mountain

by Peter Le Breton

My father was a naturalist, author and explorer, who studied the fauna and flora of many interesting parts of the world. After leaving Oxford in 1927 I came straight to a farm in the Trans Nzoia and have lived in the district ever since as a bride, mother and grandmother.

In 1932 we moved to a beautiful farm on the mountain. Seven wagons went on ahead along a rough track cleared by our neighbour, Sinclair Anderson, up a steep and rocky gradient. A 1000-gallon tank on one of the wagons took a bashing from some overhanging trees, but in spite of my amateur packing and a

Old Podo trees on Mount Elgon (podocarpus gracilior)

Wild flowers

Gloriosa

Sodom Apple

Cassia

Crotalaria

Rhamphicarpa

Gladioli

Asclepias Macrantha

Plants used for dyeing

Magatio

Gakaraku

Senecio

Indigo

two-day journey by wagon, the sum total of breakages was one wine-glass.

A house was built, bush cleared and a garden grew with – joy of joys – water running through it. The Furrow has played a major part in our existence. Our whole being is centred around it; it is our life-line, our only water supply except for rainwater carefully preserved in the battered tank's successor. It runs for four miles through forest and serves our two houses, the Andersons' and our own. Elephants are the greatest menace. Each elephant has four large feet, multiply that by 50 or so and the furrow can be wrecked in five minutes. Fallen trees, landslides, re-forestation, all play their part in choking it from time to time. But with it I can grow primroses, narcissus, primulas, marsh marigolds and the scarlet lobelia cardinalis.

At the outbreak of war my husband, formerly a Gunner, volunteered and disappeared overseas. My daughter was then aged $5\frac{1}{2}$, so I decided to start my own small school. Petrol was rationed, so all the pupils had to be boarded. Our numbers grew and the school became my life for seven years. I was lucky to secure the help of an Irish girl, Betty Webster, whom the children adored. As a result of her skill and enthusiasm, three of our pupils who went on to Kitale School in turn became Head Scholars.

One day the furrow stopped and I hurried over my French lesson and went up into the forest. A month-old elephant calf had fallen in; its mother and relations had tried to dig it out but had only succeeded in drowning the poor baby. On another occasion, my very sober and respectable servant brought in breakfast with his *kanzu* literally in ribbons. He said an animal had attacked it in the night while it was hanging in its place on the back verandah. Next morning, not only was a second *kanzu* in ruins but so were some of my baby's clothes that had been hanging on the line. We had been visited by a leopard.

Provided that our dogs are safe, I like having a leopard or two around the place, but this one seemed to have unusual habits. We put wire netting over the dormitory windows and I lay fully clothed in the dark until soon after midnight I heard the unmistakable sawing noise a leopard makes. I waited till I heard one of the empty cans I had put on the verandah being knocked over, and dashed out in time to see a young leopardess disappearing round the corner with a small rug. In the morning the smell of leopard was so strong that the dogs would hardly come out of their kennels, and sadly I decided that I would have to take steps to get my leopard removed. So one of the fathers came and built a trap, and just after dark this unusual but much-regretted visitor was dead.

Though the days of exciting animals near at hand are over – once I saw a man innocently mowing the lawn knocked for six by two fighting waterbuck – the birds have not diminished. Rosa's Turaco, the White-Headed Hoopoe, Double-Toothed Barbet, Parrots and the blue Fly-Catcher are a delight to the eye, and Robins, Thrushes and Bulbuls fill the air with song. I get a bit cross at times with the Red-Chested Cuckoo when he arrives early in March and tells me that rain is near when I know I have to wait at least another month. Of all the birds, it is the black and white Trumpeter Hornbill with its most unmusical voice that typifies for me the mystery of the forest that is so near my garden.

Butterfly and Moth Collecting

by T H E Jackson

I arrived in the district in 1924, and was too busy clearing and developing the farm to do anything else for two or three years. It was in 1927 that I, with a friend of mine, Bob Stewart, started to collect seriously. We found a most attractive rest-camp at a place called Bulumbi near Busia, and visited it many times, and then the Malaba Forest on the way to Kakamega. In the meantime I collected nearer at hand in the remnants of forest left on my neighbour's, Wreford-Smith's, farm, and on the Suam River. I taught an African to look for eggs and caterpillars, and eventually bred most of our local butterflies. From this beginning I and my friends gradually explored the various forests in Uganda, Tanganyika and on the coast.

I kept in close touch with Dr van Someren in Nairobi, the founder and first curator of the Coryndon Museum, and perhaps the greatest naturalist in eastern Africa. I learned more from him than from any other person. He was the inventor of the famous Charaxes trap which, if baited with fermenting banana, will catch most of the Charaxes in the area in which it is placed. Charaxes are the large fast-flying genus which catches everyone's imagination when they first start collecting in Africa.

Mzee Jomo Kenyatta at the Kitale Ask Show in 1968

A new development which enabled me to re-collect in all the Uganda forests was the erection by the Virus Research people in Entebbe of a 120-foot steel tower in a forest patch near Mpigi. It enabled us to collect in, under and over the canopy, and the results were astonishing. We not only got many things never before seen in eastern Uganda, but also half a dozen completely new species. Since then we have collected in other forests, building our own ladders up into the canopy, and platforms from which to collect. It is essential to choose the right tree which must have a nest in it of a particular species of ant (Crematogester), since the early stages of these butterflies are spent among the ants. So – let everyone and anyone who is interested continue to collect while there is still time and before Homo Sapiens destroys the habitats forever.

(The author, Pinkie Jackson, who was murdered on his farm in 1968, assembled one of the world's finest collections of African butterflies. He developed new collecting and breeding techniques, and trained a number of Africans to collect butterflies throughout tropical Africa. In 1961 he presented some 65 000 specimens to the British Museum. His garden was famous for its many rare flowers, and his trees became hosts to exotic and indigenous orchids. On his farm he established a thriving coffee plantation and later pioneered the growing of tea, building the first tea factory in the Trans Nzoia.)

African farmers with hybrid seed maize sold by the Kenya Seed Company in Kitale

Padre Knight

by Alan Knight

The Rev. O H Knight, who had spent 15 years in Japan as a CMS missionary, came to Eldoret in 1920 as Chaplain. He had no car at first and was constantly on safari on foot and by bicycle, covering great distances as he visited scattered farmers in their homes.

At first there was no church, and services were held in the houses of his parishioners, but he built the first church in mud and wattle, just outside what is now the DC's office in Eldoret. In 1923 he retired and bought a farm in the Trans Nzoia, but for the next 40 years continued to serve the district voluntarily.

In 1926 he imported a steam traction-engine from John Fowler in England. He and Eddy Duirs assembled it at railhead in Eldoret and then started to drive it up to Kitale. Unfortunately the rains started just then and the unhandy vehicle was constantly getting bogged down in soft ground and on ant-hills. It also took an army of men cutting and stacking firewood along the road for it, and teams of oxen to cart water. The bridges of those days were all declared unsafe for a traction-engine whose weight was ten tons, but Padre Knight crossed his bridges and argued about them afterwards. Finally, several weeks later, he drove triumphantly into Kitale pulling two five-ton trucks behind him.

In 1968 he became 93 and his wife 89. On 17 November about 60 people were invited to tea at Alan and Maud's house to celebrate the diamond wedding of their parents. The family present ranged from the three sons and daughters-in-law down to three very small step-great-grandchildren. One of the guests composed and read an ode in honour of the day.

Opposite: Kisumu town centre looking across the bay to the Maseno road and the airport, golf club and industrial area where Old Kisumu was sited

FOURTEEN
KISUMU

by J L Riddoch

The town of Kisumu was sited by Hobley on the north side of Ugowe Bay in 1900, where it was originally intended that the port should be established. When Port Florence was in fact built on the south side, in 1902 Hobley transferred the administrative and business premises to the higher and relatively healthier ridge adjoining it. However, the newly built township retained the name Kisumu.

Miss Lisette Chadwick started the first girls' boarding school in Nyanza at Sunrise, Maseno, in the year 1895.

Many interesting birds can be seen without leaving the township. In a visit to Hippo Gardens or a drive along the lake shore Fish Eagles, Hadada and other Ibis, Open-Bill Storks and Jacana can usually be seen, and Pied Kingfishers in the evening. Numerous Cormorants roost in the large gum trees. Small flocks of the Black-Billed Barbet often appear now, though it is only recently that these birds have been recorded from Kenya.

In 1950 to 1951 the Municipality undertook the pasteurization, packing and distribution of milk in Kisumu, thus establishing the only municipal dairy in Africa.

A municipal herd of impala lives along the south shore of the lake.

The sailing instructions of Kisumu Yacht Club provide that: 'nets, papyrus and hippopotami may be treated as obstructions to sea room.' They have not needed to include any mention of crocodiles.

These birds are found in the Molo and Turi area where they live at high altitudes of 7000 to 9000 feet

Top right: Black and White Casked Hornbill

Top left: Green headed Sun Bird

Left: Augur Buzzard

Right: Barn Owl

FIFTEEN
MACHAKOS AND ULU

President Theodore Roosevelt with baby cheetah. He and his son, Kermit, visited Kenya in 1909. He hunted lion in the Mua Hills and also shot some on the Kapiti and Athi Plains

In pre-colonial times Arab slave caravans en route to and from Uganda, to whom the Kamba supplied food in exchange for beads, cloth and other goods, halted at Ulu. The Imperial British East Africa Company established its first up-country station at Nzoi and then moved to Machako's, the headquarters of a chief more correctly spelt Masaku. He was said to be a big, hairy man and lived on Kilima Mimwo.

The first European in charge of the post, George Leigh, seems to have been an unfortunate choice and there was some friction with the Kamba, even an attack on the fort. In January 1892 John Ainsworth took over and stayed at Machakos until 1899, employed first by the Company and then by the Protectorate Government. He began to build a stone fort and houses, stores and barracks, but in August 1892 was informed by the Company that there was no more money, so he must evacuate Machakos. He offered to stay on without pay, and soon afterwards Sir Gerald Portal, sent out from London, recommended that the British Government should take over. So Ainsworth remained, the building was continued and in 20 months a stone fort was complete. This was in existence until 1920 when, it is said, a DC fell into the ditch and ordered the whole thing to be destroyed.

Ainsworth really made Machakos. He established friendly relations with the Kamba, imported plants and trees from Australia, laid out vegetable gardens, and won general respect for his quick, fair and firm administration of justice.

'He supplies us with seeds
and looks after out needs –
what a wonderful change
from the era of beads!'

ran a doggerel verse by some early settlers. It was he who got the first Agricultural Show put on in Nairobi on 26 February 1902.

The area chosen by the Government for settlement in Ukamba province lay in the no-man's-land between the Kamba and the Maasai, where there were more wild animals than people. Harold and Clifford Hill were the first to come. Three problems the newcomers had to face were shortage of water, difficult soil and insect plagues. These remain. Nevertheless several crops, among them wheat, citrus and coffee, have been established and cattle ranching is the major industry.

The Hills of Katelembo

by J K R Thorp

I stood in great awe of Harold Hill, my father-in-law, not so much because of his reputation with gun and rifle, but rather for his complete mastery of an environment strange to me, his forthright attitude, his inability to suffer fools gladly and his amazing store of physical energy.

Harold Hill came to East Africa at the age of 24, and in 1906 took up land in partnership with his cousin, Clifford, on the slopes of the Mua Hills, in the Machakos district. From his first mud-and-thatch homestead on a rocky knoll he could look 120 miles southwards across the game-covered Athi and Kapiti Plains to the snowy table-top of 19 000-feet-high Kilimanjaro. Born in South Africa of English stock – his grandparents came out with the 1820 settlers – Harold had served with Nesbitt's Scouts in the Boer War in 1899, and then became a Treasury official in Johannesburg. He soon decided that life among the ledgers and vouchers was not the life for him.

The Hills called their farm Katelembo after a species of lizard. One of Harold's first acts was to set a broody hen on 13 eggs. When he proudly took a visitor to see his initial farming enterprise, he found no hen or eggs, but a cobra coiled up in the nest. Harold shot the cobra, recovered the eggs intact from its insides, found the terrified hen and re-set her. It is typical of his lack of bombast that he never embroidered the story – the eggs didn't hatch.

When on a foot safari to buy cattle in 1906, the Hills had camped near Katelembo and noticed some bushes of small yellow daisies like those which grew on their father's ostrich farms in the Eastern Province of the Cape. Ostriches were feeding on them. Ostrich farming was booming then in South Africa and they decided to try it. Each cousin took up a position on a hilltop to scan the plains for newly-hatched chicks. These they caught and carried back in sacks, often with the mother bird following. Later they imported pedigree cocks and also incubators. Really good feathers then fetched as much as 35/- each.

Leopards were a major problem. When they got in among the penned birds at

FORT MACHAKO'S. 1899.

Entrance to Fort.

Quarter Guard of East African Rifles (Soudanese.)

Bottom: John Ainsworth in a rickshaw in 1915

Philip Percival (mounted) and Harold Hill

night they caused ghastly destruction. One morning in 1908, after a disastrous night, Harold and Clifford set off to follow the offending leopard, their only weapon being a single-barrelled black powder gun. They found the culprit in a thorn tree, chewing a lump of ostrich meat. Clifford fired, the leopard fell, and a Kamba herdsman poked the body with his spear. The leopard did not move, but when Harold approached, it sprang up and seized his left shoulder in its jaws. Clifford's gun jammed, and blows with the butt only infuriated the animal. Clifford seized its tail and tried to pull it off, but let go when Harold, who was being torn about violently, objected. Suddenly the leopard dropped Harold's shoulder and made off into the bush. All they could find to put on the wound was the cold tea they had brought for their lunch, with some permanganate they always carried in case of snake-bite. The wounds eventually healed.

On another occasion Harold was walking back to his camp on the Athi Plains from a shopping expedition to Nairobi, carrying only his purchases and no gun. Hearing a noise behind him he glanced round, to find he was being closely followed by a lioness and two cubs. He walked steadily on, not daring to leave the track nor look behind again. His unwelcome companions padded after him. The procession continued for about two hours, when for no particular reason mamma lion decided she had walked far enough and took the children off into the long grass. Harold said that he had never been so terrified, either before or since. When he eventually stumbled into camp he had not a dry stitch of clothing on him.

Lions swarmed in those days. Up to 1918 Harold had been in at the death of

135, and Clifford of 160. Neither was a professional hunter. No wonder some of the first attempts at cattle ranching failed.

After the Second World War a new start had to be made. Wheat was a failure owing to locusts and weeds. Harold planted oranges and coffee, and began to build up his cattle. Hunting no longer interested him. At the age of 75 he handed over Katelembo to his son Norman and 'retired' to a small piece of land, planting coffee and oranges and fencing it for cattle. He was still working full-time when he died in 1963 at the age of 82.

Ostrich farming

Guidance on ostrich farming published in 1909 shows a picture of an ostrich in a pen with its head in a sock. The feathers are cut about four inches from the skin, it says. Ostriches are nervous and highly-strung but when unable to see stand perfectly still. The stubs are left in for about six weeks to dry, after which they can be pulled out painlessly.

A Machakos childhood

(i) by Peggy Howden

Any journey was exciting when I was a child. If we had to go to Nairobi it meant leaving home in the dark in an ox-cart, with a mattress laid on its floor. We cuddled down under blankets and dozed while the drivers sang and cracked their whips. We usually reached the station, Kapiti Plains, in good time to have early breakfast before the train from the coast came in.

When we eventually reached Nairobi we were sometimes met by Ali Khan's smart buggy with a team of mules, but I liked a rickshaw best. The men set off tinkling a bell to clear a path. We usually stayed with friends who had their own private rickshaws with uniformed men and clean white frilly covers to the seats.

Going to the coast was best of all. Great preparations were made beforehand. The carriages were very dusty and Mother tied fine scarves round our heads to try and keep us clean. We loved getting out to eat at the station restaurants – tinned fruit and paper napkins were a great thrill. At dusk a man walked along the roof of the train, lighting the carriage lamps from above. Smuts from the wood-burning engine flew back and were lovely to watch when it was dark, though we used to get sparks in our eyes, and grass fires caused by the sparks were a menace.

The first sight of the sea and the journey in a rickshaw to the ferry at Freretown were also thrilling. The train went right into Mombasa where the GPO is now. A great bell ringing, shouts, passing *hamali* carts with their chanting, pushing teams of men, and all the exciting sights, fascinated me.

The reef was a paradise for shelling and when the tide covered it we came back to eat and then climb the coconut palms. We sometimes used to pool our resources and hire a canoe for 50 cents a morning and go drifting over the coral near the island. Sometimes we wandered in the village of Freretown and bought palm brooms to take home. No one sunbathed in those days. We wore our hats from 8 a.m. to 4 p.m., and rested from two to four.

Once a year we made a journey to replenish our supplies of fat, travelling in a four-wheeled ox-wagon pulled by about 18 oxen. A small urchin called a *mshika kamba* led the front pair, and the men and Father drove the team. Their rawhide whips were always looped so that they did not cut the oxen's hide when they beat them. We trekked from Potha (our farm) across the slopes of Thaki and slept our first night at a Dutchman's empty house. Next day we reached the Athi River. There was lovely shade and green grass for the oxen. Father (Philip Percival) duly shot a hippo, which was hauled to the shallows by ropes, and then he sat on the bank with a rifle in case a crocodile approached, while the men skinned the hippo, and I fished. I remember clearly chewing chunks of freshly-cooked hippo fat, which the Africans were eating. Mother rendered down as much as she had space for, and we wasted nothing of the meat or hide.

As time went on Father was away more and more, as he became a well-known hunter – he needed the money because the farm didn't pay. The cattle died in spite of all we did, and market prices for pigs, oranges, or whatever we managed to produce never seemed to cover costs of production. Mother made butter to sell in Nairobi. I can see her carefully lining the box in which it travelled with Silky Oak-tree leaves to try to keep it cool.

Water was very precious: the tin tanks which filled with rain-water from the roof were kept locked, and each week a spoonful of paraffin was poured in to stop mosquitoes from breeding. We had *posho* (maize) porridge with lovely brown jaggery sugar on it. Sometimes the Africans caught eels for us in the permanent pools, a pleasant change as otherwise we never saw fish. I think we must have been very short of fat, living on lean buck meat, as when Joy and I went as boarders to Limuru School, we were a nine days' wonder, as we would eat up all the fat which the rest of the girls hated.

During the First World War Mother was alone most of the time with only me to start with, later Joy, and later still, Dick. She had only one servant as she couldn't afford more, and it must have been hard work carrying the water up the outside ladder to the bath, as we had no piped water until after I was married in 1937. Our servant taught us how to wash our clothes using a root which produced a lather, when we had no soap during the war.

Illness was sometimes a problem and everyone had to help each other. When I had typhoid, which took a month to diagnose, Harold Hill came in his, as well as the district's, first car, and drove us to Athi River where we went on by train to Nairobi. I have never forgotten the headaches, nor the horror of Dr Burkitt's famous cold-water treatment. I had to lie on a mackintosh sheet in a draught, and of course all and sundry were going about their work and saw me naked. I nearly died of shame, let alone typhoid. I was starved as part of the cure and was so light when I got home that Dick and Joy used to push me about in a small wheelbarrow. There were tragedies, too. The Bensons had a little girl who fell into a rubbish pit with a fire smouldering in it, and died of burns. But considering the lack of knowledge and doctors, we survived remarkably well.

No one ever had a happier childhood; it seemed to me that everyone was our friend. No one came to the house who didn't stay, or at least have a meal. In the early days they had walked. Even the DC, followed by a string of porters, used to camp occasionally. It came as a shock to me as I grew older in a different part of the world to find that all the world wasn't, in fact, a friend.

(ii) by Joy Beresford Peirse (formerly Percival)

Mrs Harold Hill was expecting her first baby at about the same time as my mother, Vivian Percival, was expecting me. This was during the First World War, when all the men were away. The two lonely women arranged a signal to tell each other whether it was a boy or a girl, by hanging a red or a white blanket, as the case might be, out of the bedroom window. Apparently it could be seen, with binoculars, from Katelembo, six miles away from Potha.

Running water and inside sanitation were unthought-of luxuries. I can still smell the taste of brackish greenish-brown water, carefully boiled, which we drank in times of drought. It came from a water-hole in the dried-up Potha 'river' surrounded by a double thorn fence to keep out game and stock. Poor things! The buck used to be found dead outside the barricade, drawn by the scent of water in a parched land. It still hurts me to see a dripping tap.

And yet, how happy people were and what a spirit of friendliness prevailed! When the district gathered for one of its rare festivities or for a church service, everybody came, and things like dentistry followed the sermon. I can remember Mr Johnson, 'Uncle Charles' of the Africa Inland Mission, pulling teeth more than I can remember him preaching. There was never any friction between the different denominations. It seemed sad that this united worship ended when sufficient funds were at last collected to build a church.

Protection is afforded by a double terai

A python before breakfast

by E W

It was 7 o'clock and my husband would not be back from the morning round for an hour or two. I was bathing the baby when there was a knock on the door. A syce had come to report that there was a python among the sheep, but had not attacked yet.

I collected a 12 bore shot-gun and a .45 Colt automatic pistol and went with the syce to where the sheep were peacefully grazing. The shepherd pointed to a patch of long grass.

We advanced cautiously, peering hither and thither, until suddenly I spotted what looked like a dried-up sisal pole deep in the brown grass. As we watched, it moved. I raised the gun, took aim at where I judged the head and neck might be, and fired. The result was spectacular. An enormous column of the huge body reared into the air, writhing in knots, and then crashed out of sight into the thorny bush of the *donga*.

We decided to make a wide detour up the hill and try to see the snake from above. Luck was with us. Eventually we caught sight of the flat, diamond-shaped head, motionless on a big rock 12 feet below where we were standing. A second shot at close range finished the hunt.

The body was trundled home in a wheelbarrow. Two very excited small boys helped to stretch out the python to its full length, 14 feet 6 inches, on the lawn in front of the house. The shoes which I had made of the skin were too small and I had to hand them over to a friend.

Measuring the python

Bee-keeping

by J K R Thorp

Every Mkamba is a bee-keeper; the possession of beehives is an essential part of the tribal culture as is the possession of cattle and goats.

The Akamba beehive is a barrel made from a hollowed-out log, varying in length from about a half to one metre. The ends of the barrel are closed by flat pieces of wood which fit inside the rim. Frequently there is only one entrance and that at the centre of the owner's mark. When the hive has been constructed, seasoned, and is ready for use, it is singed inside with a bundle of lighted twigs to remove any small projections, etc., for the Akamba know that bees like the inside of a hive to be quite smooth. This is usually done with the leaves and twigs of certain trees which are aromatic, and the smell left in the hive after they have been burnt is attractive to bees.

The hive is then carried by the owner or one of his sons to the selected tree. All the work connected with bee-keeping is man's work, so that although it is usually the women who carry things it is the men who carry the hives. Women, however, often carry honey in *ngusu* (triangular skin bags) after it has been extracted.

African bees are well known for their fierceness. The Akamba, accordingly, treat their hives with a view to lessening the fierceness of the future inmates. A kind of lizard is put into the hive and a bit of honeycomb is rubbed against a bit of mutton, after which the bees are ordered not to be fierce, but to behave as peacefully as the lizard.

Certain trees are favoured for placing hives, the foremost being the baobab. Fifteen hives in one of these giants is nothing remarkable. Steps up the trunk are made, using wooden pegs. Hives are frequently put in what appear to be quite inaccessible places, and it is not unusual for a man to receive a serious injury, even to lose his life, by falling from the tree when putting up or extracting honeycomb.

When honey is to be extracted, about an hour after sunset, the tree which contains the hive is approached. It is cool. The bees have entered the hive for the night and are silent. A fire is lighted close to the tree and by its light one member of the party climbs up to the hive, taking with him a long thick rope made of baobab bark fibre. To one end of this is attached a smooth triangular piece of wood some 15 cms. long. He takes up a position (usually very precarious) close to the hive and throws down the free end of the rope, which is caught by a man waiting below. The end to which the block is attached is thrown over a convenient branch near the hive. Meanwhile his assistant below is attaching a receptacle (*kithembi* – a wooden barrel with a skin bottom and lid) to the rope. He has also prepared a bunch of thin sticks bound together, and now lights one end of this and ties it to the loose end of the rope.

The man in the tree hauls these up, takes the brand in one hand, blows on it to make it burn brightly, and moves it slowly with a circular motion close to the lid of the hive. By now the queen has been driven to the far end. When the first angry buzzing has given place to a more regular hum, the man carefully removes the lid and advances the brand to the mouth of the hive, driving any bees that remain inward. He then cuts out the first comb with a knife, shakes it to remove any stray bees, and places it in the receptacle. He repeats the process until about two-thirds of the comb has been removed. The hive is then closed, the receptacle and brand lowered, and the operator descends from his perch.

Great care is taken to leave a comb containing eggs and larvae untouched. It is very seldom that the operator gets badly stung; how well the bees are controlled, and how little feared, is shown by the fact that he usually cuts the combs from the midst of the bees, stretching his arm the full length of the hive. These combs when taken out are a solid mass of bees, which are removed by gentle shaking and scraping. During the whole proceedings very few bees perish.

Theft of honey and breaking of beehives have always been considered very serious crimes among the Akamba. The Mkamba bee-keeper is deeply attached to his bees. He respects their intelligence and marvels at their industry. He knows how to look after them and how to control them without fear. Nevertheless he is never foolhardy, and none knows better than he the potential power of these tiny creatures, a power which they will use without hesitation in defence of their homes.

SIXTEEN
MOMBASA

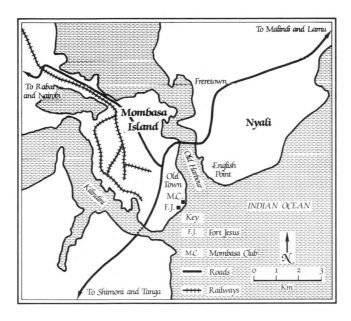

The British connection with Mombasa goes back to 3 December 1823 when two naval vessels, HMS *Leven* (Captain Owen) and the brig *Barracouta* (Captain Vidal) anchored in the harbour on a surveying expedition. The Sultan of Mombasa invited them to hoist the British flag over Fort Jesus as protection against Seyyid bin Sultan, the ruler of Oman, who was threatening the island. The British officers refused. When Captain Owen returned two months later he found the British flag flying over Fort Jesus none the less.

He agreed to transmit the Sultan's request to the British Government and, pending a reply, to leave Lieutenant Reitz in charge of Mombasa. Three months later (1824) the young officer, aged 22, died of fever and was buried in a ruined Portuguese church. The Sultan's request was refused by the British Government.

The German, Ludwig Krapf, employed by the (British) Church Missionary Society, arrived in 1844, and was joined two years later by Johan Rebmann. These two great missionaries and explorers saw Mount Kilimanjaro in 1848 (Rebmann) and Mount Kenya in 1849 (Krapf). Mrs Krapf and her new-born baby died shortly after their arrival and were buried at English Point at the entrance to the Old Harbour. Dr Rebmann started a mission at Rabai, some 15 miles inland from Mombasa, where the original church still stands.

Sir William Mackinnon, philanthropist and founder of the British India shipping line, developed the shipping industry on which the trade of eastern Africa depended. In 1885 he formed the British East Africa Association which, in 1888, obtained a Royal Charter and became the Imperial British East Africa

Company. Then came the building of the Uganda Railway. The first rail was laid on the mainland opposite Mombasa in 1896, and the last in 1901 on the shore of Lake Victoria.

Milestones
1896
by Edward Rodwell

A line of chairs on which the women sat; behind them, the men stood straight as sticks in starched white uniforms, with swords, and big white military topees. Mr George Whitehouse, chief engineer of the railway, handsome, thirtyish and frustrated, addressed the gathering. It was an historic day, he said, because the railway had been a long time coming. It would still take a long time to complete but when it was done East Africa would be changed; the old order would be gone forever. Whitehouse then signalled for the first rail to be laid.

Mombasa in 1896 was not much of a place. Ndia Kuu and Vasco da Gama Street comprised the shopping centre. There was no piped water, no sewers, no garbage collection, but plenty of flies and rats, and a cemetery with bones of the late lamented protruding from the shallow earth. Road surfaces were unmade. Used as main drains for centuries past, they stank. Most of the island was covered by jungle, infested with puff-adders, and leopards roamed about the town at night.

As to population, the jail contained 150 prisoners; there were 169 Goans and about 15 000 Africans, mainly Swahili; 6000 Asians, 500 Baluchis, 600 Arabs and 2667 slaves. Add to this the ladies and gentlemen who had watched the laying of the first rail. There were 24 Protectorate officials and their families, 39 railway employees and their families, 20 missionaries, 10 English businessmen and 2 Germans, 4 Greek contractors, and 2 hotel keepers of the same nationality, 2 Romanian hotel-keepers and 4 idlers.

There was also the new Mombasa Club and the Sports Club just opened, for which Sheikh Ali bin Salim had given land. At the former, a bell rang at 7 p.m. to signify that all women were to leave the premises. But women were allowed in for dinner on special occasions. Judge Hamilton once asked officials and their wives to dinner. The guests sat round a huge table. The Judge would not divulge the ingredients of the pièce de résistance, which was to be a surprise. It was borne into the dining room on a great covered dish and placed in the centre of the board. Everyone was agog. The host lifted the cover and immediately a hundred black, long-legged crabs scampered all over the table. Well, he was quite right. It was a surprise.

1907

Up to 1907 anyone could land from a ship without immigration formalities or even a passport. The first lighterage wharf was built that year. A meeting of Europeans was held to protest (in vain) against the removal of the seat of government from the coast to Nairobi. In September there was a great outcry

Top: Fort Jesus, dedicated in 1593, and Mombasa Club, opened in 1897. The Fort was occupied in turns by the Portuguese and Arabs, and when the British Protectorate was claimed in July 1895, it became a prison. After restoration, it was officially opened to the public on 29 November 1960

Bottom: Emmanuel Church at Freretown, the CMS mission settlement on the north mainland, was built by freed slaves in 1884. The bell was rung at night to warn dhows that the settlement was guarded, in case the Arabs were considering raiding it for slaves

from Mombasa housewives when beef reached the black market price of 25 cents (2p) a pound.

Mr Winston Churchill, Under-Secretary of State for the Colonies, arrived in HMS *Venus* for a short visit. He found no lack of commercial enterprises at the coast. There were two daily newspapers; the plant for one, the *East African Standard*, had been bought by Mr R F Meyer from Mr Jeevanjee for £50. The oldest European company on the island, Smith Mackenzie and Co., had its offices in Vasco da Gama Street. Ships still called at the Old Harbour although many were discharging at Kilindini. Shops were full.

The Agricultural Society had held its first Show at the Sports Club in 1903. Produce of all kinds was shown – crops, fruit, and 'heap upon heap of vegetables', but livestock entries were poor – only two cows with calves, and two donkeys. All along the coast plantations flourished, but not for long. The bottom fell out of rubber and copra. One by one the settlers were beginning to move up-country. But the big sisal estate at Nyali went on, under the management of Mr Rodwell. You reached it by ferry across Nyali creek. Public transport was by narrow tramlines with open trolley-cars which were pushed by hand; everyone could see what was going on and there was plenty of time all round.

1914

The First World War brought the German raider, *Königsberg*, and a German threat from the south. Soon Mombasa was the bottleneck through which moved the men and materials of war. The first motorized ferry connected the island with the south mainland at Likoni. Field guns were mounted on the seafront. Sheikh (later Sir) Ali bin Salim, Liwali of Mombasa, was a tower of strength, urging the local Arabs into the Arab Rifles; his generosity towards any fund was proverbial.

1931

After the war Mombasa continued to expand. The Roxy cinema was opened and then the Regal. The Manor and Tudor House Hotels offered a sophisticated service; a road was opened between Mombasa and the capital. Then came the blow that paralysed the world: the great depression.

With sisal at £9 a ton and coffee at round about £30; with most salaries in the £10 to £25 a month range and commerce almost at a standstill, one would think that pessimism would be complete. Not so. People provided their own amusements. It cost little to play soccer, rugby, tennis; to sail and row; you could dine on a visiting ship for a few shillings. A second-hand car could be bought for £5; petrol was 1/- a gallon. The chit system prevailed, nothing was paid for in cash. Taxation was low. Each European paid a poll tax of 30/- a year and an education tax of about the same amount – finis.

If Mombasa was poverty-stricken, it was also a happy place in which to live. Everyone, black, white and brown, was friendly and easy-going. Mombasa was a meeting-place of races. And the poverty was to pass. With the rumblings of the Second World War the economy began to pick up. Mombasa has never looked back from the fillip provided by the tragedy of the Second World War.

Dhows

Once the *kaskazi*, the north-east monsoon, is established, the Old Harbour prepares to receive the dhows. These sturdy, adventurous little craft have been coming to Mombasa since time immemorial across the Indian Ocean from Arabia, India and Somalia, transforming the Old Harbour from a sleepy backwater into a hive of activity.

There are several different kinds of dhow. Many are the large double-enders, with stem heads thrusting upwards and forwards. The rounded end of the projection is painted black with a white band, and often, near the tip, on the jackstaff, is a model aeroplane. These are the Booms which, in the main, come from Iran. Their raised poops narrow to a strong rudder post from which the rudder hangs. A tall painted flagstaff dominates the stern, and two pointed 'toilet' boxes hang from the ship's side flanking the rudder.

The Sambuks are the next most numerous. These square-sterned vessels vary according to their port of origin, but all show the stem head curving upwards from the water-line to end just above the hull, with the forward edge reaching higher than the after edge. It resembles a scimitar cleaving the waters ahead.

The Suri Sambuks have rather a broad, flat bow projection with the leading edge not far above the after edge, whilst the Red Sea Sambuks and those from the Hadramaut carry the forward edge much higher, and the sides of the projection are painted, and may carry a rounded 'oculus' in the centre, containing crossed swords or other decoration. Their sterns differ also.

The Suris have small cut-outs in the shape of stylized trees, usually two or four beneath a narrow curved transom arch, whereas the Hadrami and the Red Sea ships have decorated oblong panels on either side of the external rudder. Most Suri Sambuks have rudders which pass up a trunk to a tiller on the poop. The Suri ships usually confine coloured decorations to small areas on the quarter, using blue and white colours, whereas the others paint their quarter boards and sides in gay colours.

The most delicately carved and decorated ships are the Ghanjabs from Sur and the Kotias from India. The transom arches are usually much broader than those of the Sambuks, and looking out from the stern are five windows with curved pillars between them. Many parts of these ships are blessed with attractive carving. It is said that these are the females of the dhow fleet and therefore much care and attention is lavished upon their decoration. The Booms are their masculine counterpart.

There are several other varieties to be seen at the height of the season, including the quaint Badan or Bedeni with their tall rudders and rudder posts, the small Babnus with their masts raked far forwards, the Zarooks, and a small Baghla that is a constant visitor. Dhangis and a variety of ships that go under the general name Barig (a corruption of brig) come from India.

The dhows bring wares of many kinds for sale. Brass-studded chests are piled one on top of the other around the walls of the Customs House main hall, whilst the floor is covered with a great variety of carpets. Coffee pots and small money

The carved transom arch of this Ghanjab is shown with the five windows of its stern galleries. The carved decorations round the windows have come away over the years

boxes fill up the unoccupied corners. Milling around are merchants and visitors eager to strike a bargain, while the dhow men sit and survey the scene. There are cargoes also of salt, fish, dates and, until recently, tiles.

In the Old Harbour the dhows lie four or five abreast alongside the jetty. Stevedores carry sacks of coffee and other foods on their backs to be tipped into the holds while the ships await the change of the monsoon which will speed them on their homeward journey. Very few rely on sail these days, and the sight of a dhow moving out of the harbour in full sail with the large lateen billowed out by the wind is comparatively rare. The small coastal dhows from Lamu are an exception.

The harbour empties rapidly once the *kusi* is established, the bustle in the godowns and on the jetties dies away, and the Old Port settles down to a period of comparative lethargy until the next season comes round.

Game fishing

by James Adcock

Fishing for sport has become a major industry. The wealth and variety of the coastal fish is enormous. Malindi is famous for its sailfish, Shimoni for its marlin. Kenya has only one world record, Eric Tinworth's $110\frac{1}{4}$ lb. Cobia or Black Runner, but in the All Africa charts Kenya heads the list.

Trolling is the principal method. In the early days spoons, plugs and feather jigs were the main lures in use, but these have been replaced by honolulus, plastic squids and knuckleheads. Fish bait has always been popular and nowadays fishermen think nothing of using a 10 lb. bait, very often trolled alive on a bridle to allow the fish to keep breathing. As a result, catches are getting larger and larger and records are continually broken. Larger and faster boats, better fishing tackle and more experience all contribute to the larger catches.

The variety taken is enormous – black, blue and striped marlin, sailfish, wahoo, kingfish, tunny, bonito, dolphin, barracuda, runner, and many species of shark. Broadbill swordfish have been sighted on a few occasions. Inshore fishing is also rewarding. Numerous creeks and inlets are found all along the coastline which harbour rock-cod, snapper, grunter, bream, scavenger and kolikoli – all, besides being excellent eating, put up a worthy fight. Not good eating, but rated very high for their fighting qualities, are bonefish, springer and East Indian tarpon. Trolling with small squids or spoons is one successful method used in the mouths of the inlets. Queenfish, kingfish, barracuda, barega, garfish, torpedo and kolikoli are the most likely hauls.

The future? A number of commercial longline boats, mainly Japanese, operate off the Kenya coast. In time their large hauls of tunny and marlin must have an adverse effect on game fishing, but a far more real and immediate danger is that of pollution. The increase in oil in the sea off Kenya in the past few years has been phenomenal. If this goes on, marine life ten years from now will be as sparse as that of the Mediterranean.

SEVENTEEN
LAIKIPIA

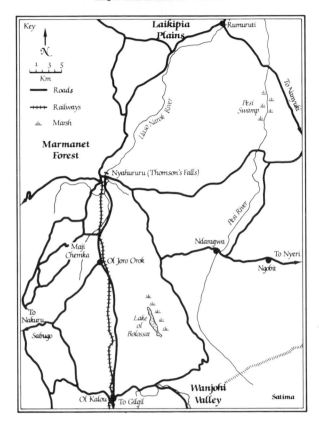

Satima, 13 120 feet high and the northern peak of the Aberdare range, or Nyandarua, is Laikipia's mountain. On its western side it falls in steep, rugged gorges to Lake Ol Bolossat, from which rise, in gentle curves, the uplands of Ol Kalou and Ol Joro Orok. On its northern side the mountain falls in gradual wooded spurs towards the vast Laikipia plains. To the east lie the foothills of Mount Kenya, majestically overlooking the whole district.

The mountain slopes are covered with dense natural forest. The Ngare Narok, rising in the Aberdares, is the main river. Just below its junction with the Equator Stream is the waterfall named after Joseph Thomson, the first white man to see its cloud of white spray hanging in the gorge 200 feet below.

The Ngare Narok and the Uaso Nyiro are the only permanent rivers. Since the region was settled in the 1920s, European farmers have created dams and sunk boreholes, often at vast expense as the water table is very low. Except in the most severe droughts, all areas can now be said to be well-watered, and land formerly considered useless can now be used for ranching cattle and sheep.

In 1883 Joseph Thomson found here a people he described as: 'Maasaispeaking but not of pure Maasai stock'. They were known as the Laikipiak by the Maasai, who invaded the area in 1890 and decimated a population already ravaged by smallpox. Then a combined epidemic of rinderpest in cattle and smallpox in humans reduced the Maasai themselves, who withdrew to their southern lands, leaving scattered remains of the Laikipiak behind.

Rumuruti

The colonial administration set up a district headquarters in Rumuruti, an onomatopoeic Maasai word for mosquito, in 1904. Mr John Collyer was the first DC, and lived there with his two sisters, Margaret and Olive, from 1905. They started the gardens that have given so much pleasure over the years.

Blocks of land ranging from 2000 to 5000 acres were surveyed in 1912 and would have been sold in 1914 but for the outbreak of the First World War, which delayed matters until 1920, when the land was given out to Soldier Settlers who drew lots for it. Rumuruti had been deserted. When the first post-war DC arrived in January 1920 (it was Mr S O V Hodge), he found the original house 'the abode of Somalis and their goats, who hurriedly poured out of the building to make way for the new owner and his brand-new wife'. The Hodges took ten days to come from Gilgil, cutting down trees to cross the streams with their mules and ox-wagon. The nearest settlers were Alex Armstrong and the Grimbeck family. Further afield were the Carnegies, the Ryans, Major Edwards, Major White and the van Zyl family. Meanwhile the first Kikuyu arrived on foot from Nyeri, the women bearing tobacco and bananas for sale.

The first store was built on Grimbeck's land in 1920, and in 1922 Jack and Ray Forrester started the European store with a combined Post Office and transport service from Gilgil. There were two ox-wagons, each with its team of 16 oxen, and in fine weather Ray Forrester made the round trip in about a week. The mail was brought by runner from Nakuru and took three days. The area was thick bush, and game of all sorts abounded – a leopard took Jack Forrester's terrier off the verandah of his *banda*.

The Laikipia Club was established in 1925 on the right bank of the Narok River, 'where elephants from the Aberdares rubbed shoulders with the club's magnificent podo trees'. There were 35 people at the first meeting, presided over by Major Cyril Luxford; the membership numbered 54. In course of time a golf-course was laid out, also a race-track and tennis courts. The streams were stocked with trout and the dams with bass and tilapia. Church services were held at the club once a month for many years. A small hospital built in the 1920s was added to over the years, and was originally in the care of Lt-Col R A Cunningham, formerly of the RAMC. Until 1925 he travelled on foot and mule-back to attend his patients, sometimes being away on a difficult case for a week at a time.

The Laikipia Farmers' Association was formed in 1920 with Alex Armstrong as the first president. In 1925 a local branch of the East Africa Women's League was formed. The first District Vice-President was the Hon. Mrs Violet Carnegie, well known for her flock of pedigree Angora goats bred for their fleece.

Subscriptions

The original subscription for founder members of the East Africa Women's League was Rupees 6 per annum, but during the (currency) trouble in 1922 it was reduced to 3/-. It was raised to 5/- in the comparative prosperity of 1927 and lowered again to 2/- in the 1930s, when it was a rule not to ask for more than 1/- for any appeal.

Legends of Laikipia *by A C*

When the north wind
Whistles through the thorn
We hear the tales of long ago
Whispering and chuckling across the years.
Legends of Laikipia,
Long before the white man came –
Lifting of stock from beyond the desert –
Long-drawn-out wars, migrations,
Laibons who foretold all that was to come.
Sagas of the men who journeyed,
Sailing from far across the seas,
Searching bravely through the unknown,
Savage, waterless land,
Seeking the snow-clad mountains,
Scanning amid the lava for the jewel-lake,
Sources of rivers meandering through arid lands,
Saving life before losing themselves in the sullen sands.

Finally, those who ventured,
Finding a life unrestricted by the claims of
Frantic civilization whose bonds
Fretted and rubbed them raw:
Forced their spirits to soar away to
'Faery lands forlorn',
Fancying they could live a life new-born.
What different legends these lives provide –
Wholly unlike those of nomad people
Who moved on and about to follow grass and water.
Some made the desert bloom, conquering in
Spite of all the hazards that beset them:
Still others used their land as a base,
Safaris took them roaming, roistering,
Sauntering, caring only to have a place to
Settle when all else had failed.
Sadly others battled on, lacking
Sufficient means and flair to wrest from a lonely place
Such a life as would fit their dreams.
They found themselves once more enchained,
Unable to escape from a life
That nevertheless gave
Them satisfaction of a sort.
In the whistle of the thorn
Every facet of the diamond that is life
Is there for the eye
Attuned to see and find.

Thomson's Falls (now Nyahururu)

The first building here was put up in the early 1920s for the Narok Angling Club, founded by Major Cyril Luxford and Captain L F King. The Narok, Equator and Pesi Rivers were stocked with trout. After the railway branch line reached Thomson's Falls in 1929, the Kenya Co-operative Creameries opened a depôt in 1931. Barry's Hotel held its first dance in the middle of that year. A diminutive Police Station was installed, then came a Post Office and the sprouting of other Government departments; also Indian *dukas*, and Andrew Dykes opened a butchery. A new township had been born.

By 1960 it had a cinema, a Dramatic Club with its own small theatre, a Country Club, three new churches, a boarding school and many beautiful houses. There was an industrial area with stores for wheat, maize, oil and petrol, several garages, three streets of well-stocked shops – one had a coffee balcony, a second butchery, and a new telephone exchange. The railway station had been enlarged to cope with the enormous crops grown by the farmers as well as the vast numbers of cattle, sheep and pigs. Large quantities of pencil slats were exported annually from the mill established in 1919 by Mr G Sandbach Baker. Pyrethrum had become a major industry and large quantities of wool were handled. Fruit, flowers, vegetables, poultry and many other 'lines' came and went. The country club had by then between 250 and 300 members, including seven Generals and an Admiral – down for the day, very likely, from 'Blood-pressure Ridge', a noted haunt of former high-ranking military personnel.

Barry's Hotel, Thompson's Falls, 1931

Settlement lottery

One man who arrived on the Soldier Settlement Scheme after the First World War found he had drawn the waterfall and gorge as his farm. Another who drew the present township reserve was so dismayed by its bleakness that, like Willie van Aardt at Eldoret, he went elsewhere.

Decoration

In the days of ox-wagons the oxen had to be branded AM and T and also PO. AM showed that an animal had been inoculated against rinderpest; T showed immunity to East Coast Fever, and PO to pleuro-pneumonia – the three major cattle scourges.

One of the old cattle traders, Fatty Garland, registered for the night at the local hotel. He noticed that the family that had registered before him consisted of a much-decorated admiral, his wife who also had several letters after her name, and their child, listed without distinctions. 'Poor little bugger', said Garland, and added after the child's name, AM and T, PO.

Ol Kalou

Early in 1903 The East African Syndicate was given a lease of 500 square miles between Gilgil and Lake Ol Bolossat. In 1916 the Syndicate commissioned Mr Stanley of Coverdale and Company to survey a number of farms for sale. The first to buy one was the artist, Margaret Collyer, sister of the DC. Soon afterwards W G Patten, an ex-DC, built a small log cabin on another of the farms. Major White started the Curragilla herd of Ayrshires with imported pure-bred cattle from Australia.

Before the advent of the railway Ol Kalou boasted one small Indian *duka*, and this was moved to the settlement which grew up round the railway station, built in 1928. By the early 1930s this tiny township had six Europeans, 100 Asians and about 300 Africans living in it. To begin with, there was game of all sorts. Elephants still trekked from the Aberdares to Sabugo, hippos from Lake Ol Bolossat explored the watercourses, and lion were plentiful.

Between Kipipiri and Satima lay the so-called 'Happy Valley', notorious in the 1920s. Most of its inhabitants had drifted away by 1939 and it became famous instead for Liduska Hornik's excellent Gorgonzola cheeses. Finally, known as the Wanjohi Valley, it was sub-divided and its farms re-settled by African farmers.

Flax was the first crop to be grown in the district. When the price dropped so catastrophically in the early 1920s the farmers turned to livestock, and later to wheat and pyrethrum. By the time Independence came there were 206 names on the voters' roll, representing about 130 European-owned farms, of an average of 1000 to 2000 acres, producing tens of thousands of bags of grain, thousands of gallons of cream, and many tons of pyrethrum.

Ol Joro Orok

Eight miles from Nyahururu on the Gilgil East road one comes to the Ol Joro Orok railway station around which a tiny township grew up. Until after the First World War no Africans lived in the district, but it is said to have lain on the Queen of Sheba's route to her silver mines at Zimbabwe. This at least was the story told by the travelling Habash (Abyssinian) and Somali traders who used to camp on Major Raynor's farm, *Maji Chemka* (Hot Springs) with their caravans of donkeys, camels, ponies and goats.

Major Raynor's daughter, Mrs Madge Onslow, recalls that the first Africans who arrived on *Maji Chemka* looking for work were three Meru, in about 1919. They hung their snuff-boxes in a tree while they started to clear the bush. With the coming of cattle, Kipsigis arrived to be employed as milkers and herdsmen. The Gilgil East road was notorious. Wagons took wool to railhead at Gilgil about once every six months. To this day there must be the remains of a splendid wagon which sank beneath the road near Hippo Bridge.

Houses were of the simplest in those early days: many a bachelor lived in 'four walls and roof'. The ordinary iron bedstead was considered a luxury. One of the most treasured items was the petrol or paraffin box, from which furniture was constructed. Each box held two *debes* which had a myriad of uses: buckets, canisters, measures, and finally, when too worn to contain goods, they were beaten out for roofing.

The horns of animals made excellent clothes hooks and hat racks; the tusks of bush-pig made good door handles. Monkey and hyrax skins were used as karosses and bed coverings. The pelts of zebra, and antelope of all kinds, became rugs. Thongs were made from strips of buffalo hide. The living room of a house built in the 1920s by Mr Jimmy Lumsden was panelled with lion skins.

Later, more substantial houses were built in brick or stone, some indeed quite luxurious. Italian prisoners-of-war introduced new standards of craftsmanship. After the Second World War many European farmers came under the Settlement Scheme of the time to develop the district, full of energy and ambition and hope for the future. It was the last considerable influx of Europeans. Most of their houses are now lived in by new African owners, a few have reverted to bush, and some have been converted into dispensaries or schools.

The Laikipiak

The original inhabitants of Laikipia, after their defeat and dispersal by the Purko Maasai, had retreated away to the north and were living as Dorobo (nomadic hunters) on the borders of Samburu country when the first Europeans came.

They are a light-hearted people, fond of dancing and singing, among the best trackers in the country, and accomplished cattle-rustlers. Here is one of the many tales they tell when they sit around their fires of an evening.

When the Laikipia Maasai first moved into the Marmanet area they found another tribe called the Loringong in possession of the grazing. The chief of these people agreed that the Laikipiak could stay provided that they undertook three labours.

First, they must boil milk without fire; secondly, clear the manyatta of fleas; and thirdly, make sandals with hair on both sides of the sole.

The leader of the Laikipiak decided that these things were simple to do.

He had a woman milk a cow very quickly into a calabash and while the milk was still frothing it was taken to the chief, who was satisfied.

Then hairs from the tails of the cattle were cut off and cut into tiny pieces and carried on leaves to the manyatta in the heat of the day; the wind caught the small bits of hair and made them hop about, and the chief thought they were the fleas which had been collected.

The third labour took a bit more thought, but eventually it was decided that if the ears of the donkeys were made into sandals they would fulfil the wishes of the chief – which proved correct.

And proved that the Laikipiak people were superior in intelligence to the Loringong.

EIGHTEEN

NYERI

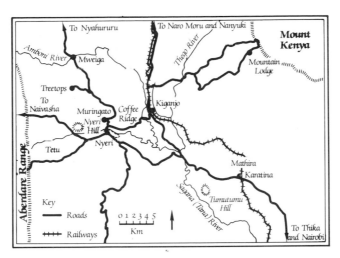

Treetops

by Joan Davies

Nyeri township, just under 6000 feet above sea level, and only 30 miles south of the Equator, lies ninety miles north of Nairobi in the fertile valley between Mount Kenya and the Aberdares. It was named by Richard Meinertzhagen in 1902 after Nyeri Hill, where he camped during an expedition against the Tetu (a branch of the Kikuyu), who had ambushed an Arab caravan.

Soon after Meinertzhagen's expedition, H R Tate started the first administrative post at Nyeri. There were Indian *dukas* in the village by 1904, and a year or two later Sandy Herd opened his general store, and then started the White Rhino Hotel. Later came the Outspan Hotel opened in 1926 by Eric Sherbrooke Walker. The Outspan operates the famous house in the trees, Treetops, where Queen Elizabeth the Second of England was spending the night when she first heard that she had come to the throne.

The idea for this hotel, first built in the fork of a huge fig tree, came from Captain Billy Sheldrick. In 1930 he was one of a party of seven Nyeri settlers who set out for Lamu on the coast, by car and lorry, by way of Isiolo, Garba Tula and Garissa, through the arid country of the Northern Frontier District, and thence down the banks of the Tana River to the sea.

On their third or fourth day out the party was ill-advised enough to camp on a rhino path leading to a swamp. Thirteen rhino went through the camp at intervals during the night. Members of the safari sleeping on their camp beds by the fire withdrew to the already crowded lorry.

A couple of days later the party pitched their tents on the banks of the Tana.

Quite close to the camp they noticed traces of many elephants coming to drink. They did not relish the prospect of another sleepless night among the larger fauna, so poles were cut and lashed to the branches of a giant thorn tree, blankets and bedding were hauled up and a hasty cold supper improvised. A full bottle of brandy was placed in the middle of the machan, and just as well.

As night fell swiftly and a full moon appeared above the branches of the thorn trees, hundreds of vast forms materialized from the shadows. Grunting, squealing, trumpeting and rumbling, they swayed down to the water. The brandy was passed from hand to hand as the party huddled together on their frail platform. For hours the great beasts drank, bathed and disported themselves, as only elephants can, just below. Then, about midnight, the whole herd vanished, as if dissipated into thin air. Seven large men on a frail platform up a tree does not make for comfort, and a most uncomfortable night was had by all.

Back in 'civilization', Billy Sheldrick said: 'I've been thinking about our night in that tree. On the edge of my farm there's a giant fig tree overlooking a salt lick and pool, where elephant, buffalo and rhino come nearly every night to drink. There's heaps of room in the tree for quite a decent-sized house, and I'm sure people would pay to stay the night and watch game.'

The idea was put to Major Sherbrooke Walker of the Outspan Hotel, who at once saw its possibilities and got to work, and the result was Treetops. It could then accommodate four to five people, and they had to walk a mile and a half through game-infested forest to reach it. The first recorded visitors on 6 November 1932 were Captain Sheldrick and his wife.

Today the tree hotel is built on a slightly different site, the Landrovers take 60 visitors per night to within 200 yards of it. The short path through the forest is well furnished with tree ladders in case of an untoward encounter.

Treetops in 1937

Marabou Storks *by P H*

Debauched amid their stinking feast,
    they gloat with lewd lasciviousness
on their abominable meal.
Behold the loathsome company –
    repellent in their greediness,
    disgustingly omnivorous,
scorned and despised by all, except
    their equally revolting mates.

Coffee Ridge

by Joy Evans

In 1911 my father and mother and their three sons trekked up to Nyeri, found their allotted farm, pitched their tent, and built a log cabin half way up the hill from the Amboni River. The railway only reached as far as Thika then. There was just a rough track, the Jambo Bwana road, taking off from Fort Hall and winding through the foothills of the Aberdare Mountains.

Nyeri consisted of a DC's camp, old Sandy Herd's *duka* and a few rondavels which were the beginnings of the White Rhino Hotel. Stakes put round the DC's camp to form a *boma* took root and a few large trees remain to this day around the club-house. Coffee Ridge was just bush and a few old *mugumu* trees, and very long grass everywhere. This had been a no-man's-land between the Kikuyu in the forest and the Maasai; the Government leased this land to European settlers to form a buffer between the two.

The First World War came, and the development on Coffee Ridge was suspended. The youngest Evans son went to France and never returned. The eldest son also went to the war and eventually came back to farm in another part of Kenya. The middle son was very badly wounded in the back and left for dead in the Tanganyika bush, but an *askari* found him and carried him back to camp. He was told he would never walk again, but sheer willpower made him throw away his crutches and walk; later he rode a horse around the shamba and even enjoyed tennis and fishing, and led an active farmer's life.

Other estates were developed on the Ridge. One of these, Seremai, had a large dam, and fishponds for breeding fish. The dam was stocked with tilapia. Later, bass were introduced and they ate the tilapia, unfortunately. Nutria were also introduced in the hope that their fur might be sold to America, but they refused to breed in captivity and escaped, causing much havoc in dams and rivers. There was also a vineyard where luscious black grapes grew in abundance. One of the pets was a cheetah, and wild cheetahs used to make their way through the coffee shambas to visit their friend in captivity. Seremai was later sold, half being kept as a farming unit and the other half divided up into residential plots and small coffee shambas, known as Chania Estates.

Back Verandah Clinic
by E J E

A man came to our house and said all the people in his village were very ill from eating bad meat. Could we help? My husband gave him a tin of mustard and a *debe* and told him to mix it well with water and make the people drink as much as they could.

Weeks after he met the same man and asked after the sick folk. The man replied it was a very bad *shauri*, and a lot of people had died.

My husband told him he was foolish to have come so many miles for treatment when he lived almost next door to the doctor at Tumutumu. 'But Bwana', he said, 'the people who took your *dawa* were all right. It was the ones that went to hospital who died.'

Smallholder tea

Nyeri was the first area of Kenya to start a smallholder tea scheme. The first tea plantings took place in 1950 in Mathira. Graham Gamble was then District Agricultural Officer and chief opponent of the sceptics who doubted the possibility of such a tea industry. Some time in the seventies the production of tea from Kenya smallholdings overtook in total amount, output from the tea gardens of the commercial companies.

Birds

by Phyllis Haynes

Nyeri has an enormous number of birds, silent for the most part during the hot weather, but when the rains begin so does the singing, led by the Chorister Robin, who rivals any Nightingale.

The Black Cuckoo calls 'Half past threeeeeee' on a melancholy rising scale, while the Red Chested Cuckoo replies 'Fish like hell' in descending notes. Burchell's Coucal bubbles delightfully with the sound of gurgling liquid, like the pouring of a decanter. He is a handsome bird, bright chestnut and black, but shy. Buntings, Larks and Thrushes, Warblers and Flycatchers are all here, and Whydah birds with their long tails streaming behind them fly over the long grass.

The Grenadiers, and tiny Waxbills, both the blue and the red, with neat brown wives, are so tame that they come on to the doorstep for their seed, Swallows fly in and out of the rooms, and build their mud nests on every corner of the house. Sunbirds flash brilliantly in the sunshine as they dip their long, curved beaks into the flowers, seeking nectar. Blue Starlings vivid as any Peacock's neck drink from the bird-bath, and Purple Starlings walk over the lawn. Shrikes and Weavers in their numerous varieties mingle with the Bulbuls, and the ubiquitous Mouse Birds devour the buds and young shoots from the garden.

Louries make flashes of scarlet as they fly from tree to tree, croaking dismally. Wagtails strut over the grass, and Kingfishers swoop along the river. Doves and Pigeons coo in the bushes, and Green Parrots fly overhead squawking like a creaking door. Eagles and Buzzards share the sky with the Vultures, and Secretary Birds and Ground Hornbills stalk majestically about, looking for snakes and grasshoppers.

Crested Cranes can often be seen flying over, uttering their curious cat-like cry. Marabou Storks gather where there is carrion, spreading their wings in the sun and sitting on their hocks. Flocks of White Ibis, on their way to de-tick some herd, shine like silver against the sky, while Green Ibis poke their long beaks into the earth for ants.

The Crowned Hornbill fly slowly and ponderously in search of ripe olives, crash-landing on the bushes, and swaying stupidly on the slenderest branch; they are the clowns of the bird world. Sparrows, of course, are ever with us, and Ducks and Geese of many kinds haunt the watersides, with Moorhen, Waders, Lily Trotters, and water birds of all sorts. Herons stand motionless, hoping for fish, and in the bush, Partridge, Bustards, Sand-Grouse, Francolin and Guinea-Fowl abound. There seems no end to the list, but this may be enough to show that Nyeri has its share of the lovely birds of Kenya.

Encounters with animals

by E A Evans

(i) The main road from Thomson's Falls to Nyeri was so bad that I turned off along a rough track which a local farmer had told me led through the forest past Ryder's, and was often passable when the main road was not. The first bridge I crossed collapsed as I reached the other side, the next one over the Pesi collapsed while I was on it, depositing my car in the river. So I set off to walk to Ryder's. It was dark by the time I got out of the forest on to the open plain. I knew the house was somewhere on the forest edge.

After a while I saw a light across the valley and thought it must be the house, so turned in that direction. The light moved away. Thinking it must be the cook with a lamp, I called on him to show me the way to the house. The only response was a rapid advance by two lions who kept me company for several hours on the open plain, their eyes showing a bright yellow light similar to that of an electric torch beam.

I was able to distinguish a belt of forest and turned in that direction, but one of the lions quite deliberately planted himself in my line of march, and turned me back towards the plain. This occurred twice. On my third attempt I marched on until within two paces of the lion, and said goodbye to myself when he crouched to spring, as I thought. But on my next step he moved aside. Eventually I reached the forest and followed a path through it.

As one of the lions was following me I climbed a tree, and the lion sat underneath the tree, his eyes fixed on me, and plainly visible in the darkness.

After a while I got cramp in the leg, and while wriggling to ease it I lost my grip and fell out of the tree just in front of the lion, who bounded away and was no more seen, while I rebounded into my tree.

After a time I descended and carried on along the path until it turned in a south-westerly direction towards Satima. Just as I was turning back I noticed a reddish beam of light across an open glade. This turned out to be a leopard, who followed me first at a distance of about 40 yards, then gradually closed up to ten yards. The red light was noticeable all the time. When I was walking away from him it lighted up the leaves on the trees, and when I stopped to look back it seemed to be flickering, as if it was focusing.

The leopard was more frightening than the lions, as he was so obviously on the trail the whole time, while the lions had been ranging round in a more casual way.

On emerging from the forest the leopard was joined by his mate, and they closed up to five yards on either side. So I made for another tree and climbed it, while the leopards took up their positions below and kept their eyes fixed on me for a couple of hours or so. At last they departed into the forest, and I was glad to see them go. Soon after I heard the most dreadful cursing and swearing from the baboons, so I expect the leopards were getting their supper from them instead of me.

I slept a while in my tree, and then as day dawned I saw the house that I had been in search of, a quarter of a mile away. I was given a nice hot bath and breakfast, and then a team of bullocks went to rescue my car which was none the worse for its dip in the river.

Before I had this adventure I thought that animals' eyes could not show light without a reflection, but this night was completely overcast without stars or moon.

by Colonel D C H Richardson

(ii) A few years ago my wife was fishing our river, the Thego, accompanied by our two Rhodesian Ridgebacks, with two puppies aged eight months. My wife landed a nice trout and was taking the fly out of its mouth when she heard the dog Ridgeback give a startled growl. About four yards away stood a large leopard poised above the dogs on the river bank, ready to strike.

Having no weapon of any kind my wife threw the fish at the leopard, hitting it in the face. At the same moment the dog puppy sprang at the leopard, which was so astonished that it turned tail and disappeared into the forest with the dogs in hot pursuit.

The fish which was to have been my supper fell into the river and swam away.

A few days later at about midday a leopard killed four of my sheep. A gun trap was set over the carcase of one of them, and the beast was killed by evening.

The leopard proved to be a very large male, the skin measuring eight foot eight inches. My wife was convinced by the size of its head and its markings that it was the leopard she had hit with a fish.

NINETEEN

NANYUKI

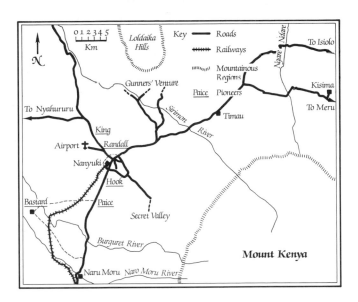

The first settlers

by Elsie Pickering

Ngare Nanyuki means 'red river' in Maasai. So it was the word 'red' that gave Nanyuki its name.

The first European settler in the district was Arnold Paice, who arrived at Mombasa on 25 April 1907. On 29 October 1910 he set off from Naivasha for the farm he had applied for with two friends, Nat Barry and Vaughan Kenealy, his kit, 13 fowls, and four dogs – his only possessions. The trio were on horseback and followed native tracks or game-paths over the Aberdare Range. They arrived at Nyeri on 1 November. Five days later they found the beacons marking the land, which contained several old Maasai manyattas, a great deal of game and nothing else.

Mr Paice introduced pigs, and sent his first batch of five to market, on foot, in September 1915. 'My pigs', he said, 'just walked and walked.' They walked to Nyeri, accompanied by one Kikuyu and three Meru, carrying maize to feed them en route; they walked across the Aberdares to Naivasha, and reached their destination, Uplands Bacon Factory, eight days after their departure, having lost in weight about 12 lbs. per pig. They fetched just under £2 each.

Old Mr Randall was probably the next to settle, closely followed by the Bastard family. There was a saying in the early days that you could not walk down the main street of Nanyuki without meeting a Bastard. Mr W S Bastard, head of the clan, came in 1912, and a son, Segar, soon after – Uncle Segar he was always called. Auntie Segar reared the first turkeys and they had to go by wagon to Thika. Uncle Segar built double-storeyed accommodation for them in the wagon, ladies upstairs and gentlemen below. Mrs Bastard senior – Grannie Bastard – made butter which she sent to Nyeri in boxes carried by runners. In 1926 she became the first District Vice-President of the Nanyuki branch of the East Africa Women's League.

Mr Bastard senior lived to a ripe old age and one day, when he was 76, announced that he was going to South Africa. His wife said: 'When are you going?' 'I'm going now,' he said. And he went. He got into his car and drove off alone. This was in the early 1920s when there were few roads, if any, between Kenya and South Africa. His only mishap was a minor traffic offence in Port Elizabeth.

Another son, Willie, sold his farm to Raymond Hook, who used to catch cheetahs for the Maharajah of Kohlapur. Helped by Maurice Randall, he lassoed them on horseback, and they fetched £25 or £30 a head. The highest cheetah speed he registered was 61 miles an hour. In 1937 he took 12 cheetahs to London meaning to race them at the White City against greyhounds, not then known to exceed 46 m.p.h., but the authorities would not allow the match.

In 1920 came the Soldier Settlers, among them Lionel and Renie Gascoigne, the Kings with their five-year-old son, Noel, and Captain John Davis. The Kings and Captain Davis set out by wagon from the New Stanley Hotel, newly opened in Nairobi. They had not gone far when a figure on a bicycle came after them, pedalling furiously. It was Lennox Murray, bringing a sunshade for Mrs King, having suddenly realised that there was no hood on their wagon.

The Nanyuki cash store in 1921

They trekked past Nanyuki and on in the direction of Rumuruti to find the 'farm' they had selected. The next months were lonely ones for Rosalie King and her small son in a two-roomed grass *banda*, while her husband and John Davis were away all day building a house and bush clearing. She was afraid to venture out of doors, for wild animals were everywhere, she was fresh from London, and everything was strange and frightening. There was no feminine company and she was often in tears. They lived on meat they shot, and canned vegetables. Their first home-grown cabbage was almost too good to eat. They looked at it for days before they could bring themselves to cook it.

Major and Mrs Gascoigne put up the first building in Nanyuki, a small shack in which they operated a contract Post Office and store. There was a manager to run it, but whenever he was away for any reason, Renie Gascoigne used to ride over on her mare, Sheila, from their farm ten miles away, through bush and forest which was alive with game, in order to run it. The farm was known as 'Gunners' Venture' as it was owned by a syndicate of ex-Gunner officers.

There were no police. They were not needed. The nearest DC was in Nyeri.

On the hoof

Yvonne Lewin was giving her first dinner party. When she went to the butcher to collect the meat he told her he was sorry but the steer had run away.

The Foxhounds and the Ostrich

There cannot be many packs of foxhounds that have been routed by one bird. This happened to the Nanyuki Hunt once, on Robin Davis' land. Suddenly the hounds stopped running and fell back. A large angry cock ostrich was the cause, prepared to defend his flock of very small babies against all comers. The grouped field had the delightful spectacle of seeing the proud, brave father bird shepherding his *totos* away whilst hounds were held back. The female bird later was seen shamefully emerging from bushes where she had taken cover.

Life with Lions

by Helen Cleland Scott

Most of my early life seemed to centre around lions. One of the first pairs we had were called Adam and Eve. One day they were left shut up in our sitting-room and I returned home to find all my newly covered chairs and curtains hanging in shreds. On another occasion, when out on safari. I was confronted early one morning by a stark naked bearer running up calling out for blankets. I immediately concluded that my husband had met with a hunting accident. However, I discovered that the bearer had parted with his blanket to wrap up the first of seven baby lion cubs my husband had just captured, and he wanted all I had with me for the others. When we returned home with the seven cubs, my precious turkeys were turned out of their house to make way for the intruders who were to dominate the next two years of our life until eventually five went to the Edinburgh Zoo and two to Rangoon.

Arrival at Kisima

by Will Powys

I arrived early in 1914 and went by train to Naivasha to an old friend, Nat Barry, who had invited me to stay. At Naivasha the Station Master said he'd had a note from Barry asking the engine driver to stop the train by the Eburru track. There the guard pulled out my trunk and chucked it into the *leleshwa* bush. The train then rushed on leaving me sitting on my trunk. It was approximately 5.30 p.m.

I viewed the country with Lake Naivasha to my left and large yellow fever trees all around. It got darker and darker. Eventually I saw car lights up on the Eburru hills. These came slowly, slowly down – at last Nat Barry arrived. He had been stuck in the mud for ages.

Barry lent me a mule to go and look for a job on the Kinangop. Here I met a wild-looking man, Seymour, on a motor-bike. He gave me a job at once, for my keep, but he did not like it much because I eat a pot of jam a day. I spent my time digging wells for windmills. Another job I had to do was to collect all stray animals – camels, cattle, donkeys, etc., and shove them through a gate on to a Goverment farm. This was to annoy Mr Macdonald, the manager, with whom he was having a row over a wool press. I was not supposed to go over there nor meet him, but I did, and asked him to find me another job as he was just off to a show at Eldoret. He did this. It was a job on the EA Syndicate, whose land stretched from Gilgil to Thomson's Falls. I was on the Syndicate until my brother, Llewellyn, relieved me so I could join the East African Mounted Rifles at Namanga.

On my return from the war I went to Galbraith Cole at Gilgil until 1925, when I left for my own farm, Kisima, which I had drawn in the Soldier Settler scheme. Lennox Murray had been there and told me all about the area. He said you could meet a polar bear there, it was so cold.

I bought a Merryweather wagon and 20 AM and T oxen from Joyce and

Wilson, loaded the wagon with a sheep dip, wool press, chickens and all my possessions, and sent it on ahead of me towards Meru. When the oxen were outspanned at Naro Moru, the drivers went exploring and so did the oxen, who were found two weeks later in the Moyo Swamp.

From Naro Moru it took us three days to get to Beale's. The oxen and wagon had to cross the wall of a dam which Beale had just made. The driver was so afraid of going into the dam that he drove the wagon over the edge the other side and it landed upside down in a gulley, wool press cracked, all the cattle on top chained together, and chickens everywhere. Nothing was broken, not even a plate.

I drove up 1200 sheep that Sandy Armstrong had bought for me from Somalis down the Narok River. It rained all the first night after they reached Kisima and in the morning over 200 were dead. I had to hurry them to the warm country, so went to see Tom Parminter's uncle and asked him if there was any low land for sale. He put me on to a farm on the Ngare Ndare belonging to a DC, so I rented it as it was empty, and put the sheep there.

I then went back to work for Cole and put my nephew Theodore in to run Kisima for about 18 months.

The Randall Clan

by Bill Randall

My father, the late J H Randall, first visited British East Africa in 1910. He decided to sell his property and move there with his flocks and family. The advance party, consisting of my late brother, Leslie, together with Mr Gush and Alton Forrester, arrived in Mombasa in 1911, bringing stud Merino sheep and horses. Unfortunately they stayed too long at Nakuru and lost a lot of the sheep. Father and Mother together with seven of the children arrived in December 1912 with wagons and gear and the rest of the Forrester family. I was 11 years old.

As we were the first Europeans to travel from Gilgil to Mount Kenya by ox-wagon, we had to make a track. I seemed either to be leading a stubborn horse or cutting thorn trees with an axe that was too heavy. Unfortunately the safari was marred by the death of Mr Gush from blackwater fever.

I believe my sister, Olive, and brother, John, were the first Europeans to be born in the district. It was quite impossible for the children to get to school in Nairobi, so back we went to South Africa in 1916, leaving Leslie to look after the stock and Cliff to fight in German East Africa, as it was then called. In 1918 my parents had had enough of South Africa so we all returned to Kenya. In 1920 Cliff was granted a Soldier Settler farm, Cedarville. My father bought the adjoining farm later owned by Jim Trench. From the late 1920s until my father's death in 1937 the Randall clan were all, except for two sisters in Nairobi, living in the Nanyuki district – Father, Mother, eight brothers and four of the sisters. Today, alas, only those left in the cemetery remain in the district.

Changes in the Game Population
by Raymond Hook

Although I bought my present farm in 1912, at the age of 20, it was not until 1919 when my war service was over that I was able to study the game. What struck me most was the number of zebras – in companies, in battalions, in army corps. The Naro Moru plains had their army corps. I remember them once on the march all travelling in the same direction, and the air seemed to vibrate with their foolish, monotonous call, 'Weh heh, weh heh'. And Angata Werhoi, the north-eastern plain of Laikipia, had quite incredible numbers. Fate was not kind to this exuberance of equine life. The farmers did not like them, they ate too much and used their intelligence to find superior grazing. One could see them scenting the wind and then they would set out for a place where rain had fallen and the grass was at its best.

In the 1920s a market was found for their hides and every Dutchman who was out of a job set out to shoot them. I rode one day with the best horseman and he killed 42, about his average for a day's hunt. In the Second World War Kenya found a home for 80 000 Italian prisoners and every one of these had to receive one pound of meat every day. Zebra, oryx, eland and hartebeest supplied the bulk of this mass of meat. And now, of all the army corps of zebra, only a few small formations remain. One company escaped persecution by passing through the forest belt of Mount Kenya and taking up its existence in the cold inhospitable moorlands at about 12 500 feet.

In 1919 many lions lived on the outskirts of this great mass of zebras and controlled their numbers with great efficiency. Lions do not go well with cattle ranching, and the ranchers got to work with poison, traps and guns, and speedily reduced the numbers. Eland were sadly depleted to feed the Italians, and the survivors suffer from periodic outbreaks of rinderpest. Buffalo have been kept in check by fairly heavy shooting. The farmers had a Game Control Club to which they contributed a cess based on each member's acreage. This was used to pay bounty of 1/- per tail of zebra, oryx and waterbuck.

The hartebeest of the Nanyuki area, a sub-species of Jackson's hartebeest, was almost exterminated to feed the Italians, but since, it has been looked after with some success and seems at present (1967) to be in no immediate survival danger.

Rhinos have decreased immensely. Years ago all the open country of Nanyuki had a sparse but well-spread population of plains rhino. All have gone. Leopards also have become very scarce. The impala is the most successful of the smaller antelope in maintaining its numbers.

As I look back over this long period, it seems that the settlers have dealt with quite gruesome efficiency with the two species they most disliked, zebra and lions. By a form of neglect, they allowed most of the rhino to be killed off. But with these exceptions, the game has been treated on the whole with a kindly tolerance. It is to be hoped that in 50 years' time the same can be said.

(Mr Raymond Hook, famous white hunter and world authority on cheetahs, died at Nanyuki in 1968 at the age of 76.)

When the Secret Valley Lodge was opened on 7 August 1961 by the Governor, Sir Patrick Renison, it was decided as part of the ceremony to release a rhino brought in a crate by Mr Carr-Hartley. When the Governor opened the crate door the rhino did not run off into the bush as expected. Sir Patrick, Major Grimwood, Air Commodore Howard-Williams, Mr Carr-Hartley and Mr Shamsu Din were marooned for some time

GLOSSARY

askari: soldier or policeman

banda: small building of temporary materials

boma: enclosure, especially for livestock; also Government administrative centre

Boran: local breed of hardy humped cattle

box-body (car): pick-up with enclosed rear portion

bundu: the bush

bwana: Mr 'The bwana' normally meant the male head of a (European) household

cattle-dip: trough filled with insecticide solution through which cattle are driven to rid them of ticks

dak bungalow: building (at railway station) for rest and refreshment

dawa: medicine

debe: 4-gallon petrol or kerosene tin used as general purpose container and measure; often beaten out flat to be used as roofing material

donga: gully, water-course (often dry), wadi

double terai: old-fashioned hat with double layer of felt as protection against the sun

drift: unbridged crossing of road over stream or donga

duka: shop

EAWL: East Africa Women's League. The name does not imply that members are drawn from Tanzania and Uganda as well as Kenya – only that Kenya was called the British East Africa Protectorate when the League was founded

fundi: skilled worker

furrow: artificial channel to lead water from a stream

hamali cart: shafted two-wheeled handcart

Harambee: modern Kenya's national motto – an injunction to pull together. It is an action-word used by groups of people pushing vehicles out of mud. Harambee secondary schools etc. are those started by local co-operative self-help groups

HE: normal colonial abbreviation for the Governor (His Excellency). c.f PC and DC for Provincial Commissioner and District Commissioner

jigger: small flea, the female of which burrows under the skin

kanzu: long-sleeved ankle-length gown

KAR: King's African Rifles

kaross: mantle of skin with the hair or fur still on, also used as bed covering

kazi pesi: quick work

kikapu: woven basket

laibon: among the Maasai and related peoples, leader with administrative and priestly duties

leleshwa: a tough bush of the savannah

liwali: an official, usually an Arab, appointed by the Government to deal with Muslim affairs

mabati: corrugated iron

machan: platform in a tree

maji: water

manyatta: temporary encampment of Maasai or related peoples

memsahib: Mrs. 'The memsahib' normally meant the female head of a (European) household

moran: member of warrior age-group

moto: fire

Mountains of the Moon: the Ruwenzori Range on the Uganda/Zaire border

mugumu: wild fig-tree

murram: a reddish-brown earth quarried and spread on dirt roads to give them an improved surface

naartje: fruit similar to tangerine

obsidian: black volcanic glass

ochre: a red clay

posho: maize-meal; a staple of many Kenya peoples

punda milia: zebra

pyrethrum: a cultivated daisy, the powdered heads of which are used to make an insecticide

ram (or hydram): a kind of pump that uses the power of falling water to raise water from a stream

rondavel: round thatched hut

rupee: the former unit of currency in Kenya; it was replaced by the florin in 1920 and then by the shilling in 1921

safari: journey, used especially of an equipped expedition into the bush

sanji grass (also ithanji): swamp plant used for thatching

shamba: plot of cultivated ground, garden, farm

shauri: plan, advice, discussion, affair

shuka: sheet-like garment

simba: lion

sisal: spiky plant from which fibre is extracted to make baler twine etc.

spine-pad: cloth flap once worn to protect the neck from the sun

sufuria: metal cooking-pot

Swahili: Coastal people whose language has become both the official language of modern Kenya and the lingua franca of much of East Africa as far as the Shamba province of Zaïre

toto abbr. mtoto: child

Thika Tramway: branch line of the Uganda Railway built from Nairobi to Thika and later extended to Nanyuki. The Governor of the day was refused funds for a railway but obtained them by the device of calling the project a tramway

Uhuru: Independence

wattle, black: fast-growing tree of Australian origin providing good firewood; tannin is extracted from the bark

INDEX

Aardt, W van 101, 140
Aberdare Mts. 35, 52, 61, 64,
    137, 138, 141, 143, 145, 149
Abraham, Jasper 93, 95
Abu Bakr 107–109
Adcock, James 135
Aden, Farah 25
Africa Inland Mission 148
Aga Khan, H H and the Begum 18
Ainsworth, John 119
Alexander, G 95
Ali bin Salim, Sheikh 130, 132
Ali Khan 16, 123
Alliance Girls' High School 48
Alliance High School 44, 46–47,
    48, 51
Allison, D M S 84
Allison, Stuart 85
Allison, Willie 82
Ambassadeur Hotel 15
Amboni River 145
Anderson, Sinclair 111, 113
Appleby, Mrs 186
Archer, Kenneth 42
Archer, Sir Geoffrey 41, 108
Armstrong, Alex 138, 151
Arnoldi 99
Arthur, Dr J W 46
Athi Plains 20, 120, 122
Athi River 35, 48, 124
Atkinson brothers 87

Babu Ram 79
Bagge, S S 62
Baillie, Frank 78
Baker, Mr 103
Baker, G Sandbach 140
Baker, Sir Herbert 75, 76
Balletto, Dr 88
Bamboo Forest 68
Baringo 108
Barker, Mr 103
Barlow, A R 46
Barnes, Mrs Lizzie 38, 53
Barnett, John 96
Barry, Nat 65, 149, 150, 190
Barry's Hotel 140
Bastard, W S 150–151
Bastard family 150–151
Belvedere Estate 49–50
Benson family 124
Benuzzi, Felice 88
Berkeley-Matthews, Mr 49
Beverley, Mrs 82
Blackett, Mt 87
Bladen-Taylor, R 49
Blixen, Baron von 25, 75

Blixen, Baroness Karen von 25,
    38, 75
Blue Posts Hotel 54, 55, 56
Blundell, Sir Michael 78
Blunt, Admiral 84
Boedeker family 13
Bogoria, Lake (Hannington) 78
Bosca, Father 59
Bowles, Dr Roger 82
Brackenhurst Hotel 31–32, 34
Breda, Bon van 98, 102
British East Africa 20, 33, 52, 151
Bruno, Fr R 59
Buchan-Sydserff, A 70
Bull, Emily 94
Bulpitt, Major 38
Bunyoro 27
Burkitt, Dr 22, 67, 124
Burnell, C B 64
Burnt Forest 99
Burrows, Eric 58
Bursell, Ake 38
Bursell, Margit 38
Busia 114
Busoga 27, 108
Buxton, Cara 87
Buxton, Clarence 30
Buxton, Hubert 88
Buxton, Sir Victor 29

Caine, W H 29, 33, 34
Cairo, 41, 42
Cameron, Mrs 76
Campbell Black, Tom 27–28
Cane, Mrs Hudson 29, 34
Carnegie family 138
Carr, Ernest 47
Carr-Hartley, Mr 155
Carver, John 39
Chadwick, Lisette 117
Chania Bridge (Thika) 51
Chania River 35, 55
Charters, Dr 44
Chege 20
Cherangani Hills 107, 109, 111
Chillingworth, T 66
Chiromo 40
Chogoria 46
Church of Scotland Mission 45
Church of the Torch 44
Church Missionary Society 20, 21
Churchill, Sir Winston 16, 132
City Park 18
Clarke, Audrey 92
Cloete, A 98
Cloete, Mrs A 102
Cloete, C Valerius 116

Cobb, E Powys 65, 93, 94, 95,
    112
Coldham, Philip 37
Cole, the Hon Berkeley 66, 181
Cole, Lady Eleanor 66
Cole, the Hon Galbraith 66, 67,
    151
Collyer, John 138
Collyer, Margaret 138, 141
Collyer, Olive 41, 138
Colville, Gilbert 66, 67
Colville, Lady 67
Cooper family 20–21
Corbett, N E F 102
Coryndon, Sir Robert 111, 114
Cowie family 52
Cowie, Mrs 15
Crake, Eric 94
Cranworth, Lord 87
Cross, Mr 95
Cullen, C D 96
Cunningham, Lt Col R A 138

Dagoretti 25, 43, 44, 46
Danby, George 95
Dar es Salaam 98
Davies, Joan 143
Davis, Capt 146–147
Davis, Robin 151
Deering, Dr 67
Delamere, Lord 20, 42, 47, 66,
    87, 93
Delamere, Lady 36, 37
Deloraine 76
Devshanathoo, Mr 29
Dick, Mr 108
Din, Mr Shamsu 155
Dobbin, H 64
Donyo Sabuk 39, 41
Drews, Elizabeth 18
Drought, Maj Jack 87, 89
Dugmore, Capt 14
Duirs, Eddy 116
Dundori 67
Dykes, Andrew 140

Eames brothers 78
EA Airways 28
EA Mounted Rifles 34, 151
Eburru 64, 66, 150
Eckstein family 79
Edwards, Maj 138
Eldama Ravine 21, 97, 98, 102,
    108, 109
Eldoret 88, 97, 101, 102, 103,
    104, 106, 111, 115, 140, 150
Elgeyo 99

Elgon, Mt 97, 99, 107, 108, 109, 110
Elizabeth, HM Queen 143
Elkington family 19, 20, 55
Elliot, Mrs 15
Ellis, Cpl (later Sgt) 14, 15
Ellis, John 37
Elmentaita, Lake 66, 67, 108
Ensoll, Jack 96
Entebbe 115
Equator River 140
Evans brothers (Londiani) 87
Evans, E A 147
Evans family (Nyeri) 147
Evans, Joy 145
Evans, Mr 15, 20

False Ithangas 57
Felix and Favre, Messrs 36
Fey family 64
Findlay family 36
Fitzgerald, Terry 82
Fools' Valley 57
Forrester family 151
Forrester, Jack and Ray 138
Fort Hall (Murang'a) 35, 36, 58, 145
Fort Jesus 129
Fort Smith 13, 27, 44
Francis, E Carey 47
Freretown 123
Freyburg, Fritz 85
Furse, David 95

Gailey, Maj J H 19, 21
Gailey and Roberts 19, 106
Galton-Fenzi, L D 40
Gamble, G 146
Garba Tula 143
Garissa 143
Garland, Fatty 140
Gascoigne family 150–151
Gethin, Capt 40
Gethin, Dick 94
Gichero, Kariuki 95–96
Gichuru, the Hon J S 48
Gikammeh 73, 74
Gilgil 20, 66, 67, 138, 140, 141, 151
Girouard, Sir Percy 64
Gladstone, Capt Tony 41–42
Gledhill, Mr 58
Good, Mrs 53
Goodwin 76
Grant, the Hon E L 55, 73
Grimbeck family 138
Grimwood, Maj 155
Gush, Mr 151

Haggie, Mr and Mrs 106
Hajee, Juma 102
Hall, Capt Francis 13, 108
Hall, J S 36
Hamilton, Judge 130
Hannington, Lake (Bogoria) 78
Happy Valley 141
Harries family (Njoro) 74
Harries family (Thika) 51–53
Harrison cousins 20, 21
Harroway, N 59
Haynes, Phyllis 146
Heard, Dr 102
Hearl, Major 59

Hell's Gate 61
Herd, Sandy 143, 145
Hewett, Sir John 33
Hewett, Lady 61
Hill, the 14–16
Hill, Clifford 120, 122–123
Hill, Harold 120, 124
Hill, Mrs Harold 125
Hill, J K and Mrs 62–63
Hill-Williams family 94
Hindlip, Lord 87
Hinga, Bernard 46
Hippo Bridge 141
Hirji, Jamal 54
Hirtzel, Mrs 30
Hobley, C W 117
Hobson, Mr 66
Hodge, S O V 138
Hoey, Cecil 98, 102
Höhnel, Lt von 77, 78
Holmes, Reggie 76
Homer, Dr 45
Hoogterp, 75
Hook, Cmdr Logan 154
Hook, Raymond 146, 152, 154
Hopcraft, J D 63
Hornik, Liduska 141
Howard, Margot 29
Howard-Williams, Air Commodore 155
Howden, Peggy 123
Hughes, Mrs Dorothy 104
Hughes, Veronica 22
Humphries family 106
Hyrax Hill 69–70

Imperial Airways 25, 27, 42
Imperial British East Africa Company 13, 43, 45, 119, 129
Isiolo 143
Ithanga Hills 57

Jackson, T H E 114, 115
Jeevanjee, Mr 16, 132
Jinja 21
Johansen, A B 58
Johnson, L A 125
Johnstone, Sir Harry 78, 108, 109
Joubert, Abraham 103
Joyce, Maj 151
Juja 39–40

Kabete 20, 21, 41, 44, 108
Kabras 108
Kacheliba 108
Kakamega 102, 103, 114
Kakuzi 59
Kalimoni 38
Kamiti 36
Kamiti River 36, 53
Kampi ya Moto 108
Kapenguria 85
Kapiti Plains 120, 123
Kapsabet 101
Karamaini 51, 52
Karen 25–26
Karuna 102
Katelembo 120, 122, 125
Kedowa 87
Keeling, Dorothy 76
Kenealy, Vaughan 149
Kenya, Mt 20, 57, 129, 137, 143, 151, 152

Kenya Auxiliary Air Unit 28
Kenya Meat Commission 82, 106
Kenyatta, H E Mzee Jomo 46, 106
Kenyatta, Margaret Wambui 46
Keringet 93, 95
Kericho 51, 88
Keyser, Maj 109
Khartoum 41, 42
Kiambu 24, 35–36, 41, 51
Kiano, the Hon Dr J 48
Kibwezi 44, 45, 108
Kidston, Lt Cmdr Glen 42
Kihumo church 43
Kikuyu (language) 33, 34, 46, 57, 73, 92
Kikuyu (place) 20, 43, 44, 45, 46, 49, 50
Kilimanjaro, Mt 20, 120, 129
Kilindini 31, 132
Kiltannon 37
Kinangop, Mt 51, 61, 66, 67
Kinangop plateau 35, 150
Kinangop, South 64, 67, 68
King, Capt L F 140
King family 150–151
Kingsford, Cicely 32–33
Kinyanjui, Chief 13
Kipipiri 141
Kipkabus 95, 96, 97
Kirawa 20
Kirk family 102
Kisii 52
Kisima 150, 151
Kisumu 41, 42, 51, 87, 117
Kitale 85, 107, 109, 111, 113, 116
Kitito Mission 59–60
Knight family 116
Knight, Rev O H 109, 116
Knight, W E D 33–34
Kogeria 37
Kohlapur, Maharajah of 150
Krapf family 129

Laikipia 77, 137–142, 152
Lake Hotel 63
Lamu 85, 143
Langata 27, 28
Langmor, Mr 15, 20
Leakey, Canon and Mrs 20, 34
Leakey, Douglas 20
Leakey, Dr Louis 20
Leakey, Mrs Mary 69
Lean, Col 85
Le Breton, P 111
Leigh, George 119
Leslie, Miss 104
Lessos 104, 115, 122
Lewin, Y 151
Likimani, Dr Jason 20
Likimani, Paul 20
Likoni 132
Limuru 29, 33, 34, 49, 51
Limuru Girls' School 124
Lindstrom family 74
Lister, Margaret 32
Loltiani, Mt 89
Londiani 87–90, 104, 110, 111
Londiani Hotel 87
Longonot, Mt 61
Lourenço Marques (Maputo) 98
Low, Archdeacon 37
Low, Mrs E M 26

Lugard, Lord 43, 76, 106
Lumbwa 51, 95
Lumsden, Jimmy 142
Luxford, Maj C 138, 140

Maasai (language) 25, 61, 109, 137, 138, 149
McCrae brothers 66
Macdonald, Mr 150
McDonell family 34
McGregor, A 87
Machakos 21, 108, 119, 120, 123
McKenzie, Mrs 27, 82
Mackinnon, Sir William 129
McMillan, Sir Northrup and Lady 39–41
McNab Mundell, J 101
McNaughton family 25, 26–27
McQueen family 26–27
Maddicks, Capt 107
Madhavji, Nathoo 66
Maji Chemka 169
Maji Kiboko 58
Major, Mr and Mrs 29
Makuyu 51, 55, 57, 59
Malaba Forest 114
Malewa River 62, 63
Malindi 87, 135
Manera 66
Marakwet 102
Marindas 96
Marmanet 77, 142
Martin, J R 25
Marula 66
Marylands Estates 79
Masara 19–20, 93
Maseno 47, 117
Matano, the Hon R S 48
Mathira 146
Mathu, the Hon E W 48
Mau, the (plateau and escarpment) 62, 65, 73, 93
Mau Summit 87, 109
Mbagathi River 27
Meinertzhagen, R 70, 143
Menengai 70, 72, 76
Meru 141, 151
Meyer, R F 103, 132
Millington, E N 95
Milne, Mrs 66
Milton's Siding 79
Mitford Barberton, R 109
Mitubiri 57
Moiben River 109
Molo 93–96
Mombasa 14, 16, 26, 28, 39, 44, 85, 98, 103, 107, 123, 129–136, 149, 151
Money, R 58
Morendat River 108
Moroto 109
Mostert, Capt 28
Mountains of the Moon 88
Mousley, B 104
Moya Swamp 151
Mpigi 115
Mua Hills 120
Mugo wa Kibiru 54
Muigai, James 46
Muguga 43
Muigai, Peter 46
Mumias 21, 108

Mundell, J McNab 119
Mungai, the Hon Dr N 48
Murang'a 35
Muringato 175
Murray, Lennox 150, 153
Museum National (formerly Coryndon) 114
Mweiga 95

Nairobi 13–18, 20, 24, 25, 26, 28, 30, 31, 32, 34, 35, 36, 38, 39, 40, 41, 46, 49, 51, 52, 53, 54, 55, 57, 58, 61, 62, 66, 67, 72, 88, 107, 108, 111, 114, 120, 122, 123, 124, 130, 143
Nairobi River 108, 146, 153
Naivasha 51, 61, 62, 63, 64, 65, 66, 98, 108, 149, 150
Naivasha, Lake 51, 150
Nakuru 62, 67, 69, 70, 72, 75, 76, 80, 81, 82, 84, 85, 86, 98, 103, 108, 138, 151
Nakuru, Lake 69
Namanga 151
Nanyuki 51, 149, 150, 151
Naro Moru 66, 96, 151, 152, 190
Narok River 138, 140, 151
Ndabibi 66
Ndarugu Heights 51
Ndarugu River 53
Ndarugu Valley 39
Nettlefold, Mr F N 41
New Stanley Hotel 21, 150
Ngala, the Hon R J 48
Ngare Waroke 137
Ngare Ndare River 151
Ngong 21, 25, 38, 48
Ngong Hills 20, 25
Nicholas family 49–50
Nicholson, Mrs M 80
Nile, River 41, 42
Nimule 41
Nivison, Cmdr and Mrs 34
N'Jibini 64
Njombo 73
Njonjo, the Hon C 48
Njonjo, Senior Chief J and Mrs 20
Njoro 73, 75, 93
Norfolk Hotel 15, 19, 34
Nyagah, the Hon J J M 48
Nyahururu (Thomsons Falls) 140, 141
Nyali 132
Nyanza 117
Nyasaland (Malawi) 45
Nyeri 46, 51, 54, 59, 138, 143, 145, 146, 147, 148, 149, 151
Nyeri Hill 143
Nyoike, Mrs Kimani 46
Nyongara River 44, 45
Nzoia River 107, 109, 110, 111

Ojal, Joel 47
Ol Bolossat, Lake 137, 141
Ol Donyo Mara 79
Ol Joro Orok 137, 141
Ol Kalou 137, 141
Ol Momoi Sidai 77
Oloo, Ald Alex 106
Onslow, Mrs Madge 141
Ortlepp, Mrs 103
O'Shea, T J 106
Otiende, the Hon J D 48

Outspan Hotel 143–144
Owen, Capt 129

Paice, Arnold 149
Parklands 15–18, 52
Parminter, Tom 151
Paterson, John 45
Patten, W G 141
Pease, Sir Alfred 152
Peirse, Mrs J B 125
Pell-Smith, D H 94
Penn, Ken 76
Peoples
  Arabs 119, 132, 143
  Asians 15, 16, 29, 31, 37, 130, 141, 143
  Baluchis 130
  Dorobo 85, 101, 109, 142
  Goans 130
  Kabras 128
  Kamba 44, 119, 120, 122, 127–128, 150–152
  Kikuyu 13, 15, 21, 35, 36, 43, 44, 46, 52, 56, 73, 74, 89, 108, 138, 143, 145, 149
  Kipsigis 87, 93, 141
  Konye, Ol 127
  Laikipiak 138–139, 142
  Loringang 138–139
  Maasai 15, 20, 21, 25, 27, 44, 62, 67, 70, 77, 93, 95, 97, 107, 108, 109, 120, 138, 142, 145, 149
  Meru 46, 149
  Nandi 98, 99, 106, 108
  Nubians 108
  Pokot 109
  Samburu 142
  Sirikwa 7, 115
  Somali 25, 138, 141, 151
  Swahili 29, 130
  Teta 143
Percival family 124–5
Percival, Philip 124, 146
Pereira, A 49–50
Perry, D 54
Pesi River 140, 147
Petrie, Tom 73
Pezzoni, Father 60
Pharazyn, Marjorie 110
Pickering, Elsie 149
Pike baby 72
Pirie, Major 49
Pioneer Mary (Walsh) 70
Plateau, the, see Uasin Gishu
Polhill family 67–68
Popatlal, Mr 50
Port Elizabeth 146
Port Florence (Kisumu) 51, 117
Portal, Sir Gerald 119
Potha 124, 125
Powys, Llewellyn 151
Powys, Theodore 151
Powys, Will 65, 150
Preston, R O 14
Price, Rev P 95
Punda Milia 57–58
Purkiss, Capt 44

Rabai 129
Rainey, Paul 64
Ramsden, Sir John 66
Randall family 150, 153–154

Ravine, see Eldama Ravine
Raynor, Maj 141
Rebmann, Johann 129
Red Lion 38
Reitz, Lt 129
Rejaf 41
Renison, Sir Patrick 155
Rensburg, Jansen van 98, 102
Rhino Park 27
Richardson, Col D C H 148
Riddoch, J L 117
Ridley, Mervyn 55, 57
Rift Valley 61, 62, 67, 78, 84, 93, 97
Ringer, Major 39
Risley family 59
Rodwell, Edward 130
Rodwell, Mr 132
Rongai 29, 72, 76
Roosevelt, Col Theodore 40
Rosslyn 21–22
Rothschild, Lord 63
Ruera River 39
Ruiru 18, 35, 38, 51, 53
Rumuruti 138, 151
Russell, T 36
Rutherfoord, Ernest 57, 58
Ryan family (Laikipia) 138
Ryan family (Molo) 95–96

Sabugo 141
St Alban's Church 95
St Andrew's Church 46
St Francis' Church, Karen 26
St Paul's College 29
Satima 61, 137, 141, 148
Schofield, Mr 106
Sclater, Maj 108
Sclater's Road 98
Scott, Clement 45
Scott, Helen C 150
Scott, Henry 45–46
Scott, Lord Francis 76
Secret Valley 155
Selfe, Mrs Mary 70
Sequeira family 59
Seremai 145
Segoit 99, 102
Seth-Smith, Donald 57
Sewell, Billy 75
Seymour, Mr 150
Seyyid bin Sultan 129
Shaw, J C 101–102
Sheba, Queen of 141
Sheikh Othman 45
Sheldrick, Capt Billy 143–144
Simam, Samuel 106
Sisal Ltd 57–58
Smith, Maj Eric 13, 44, 47

Smith, H S 87
Smith, James S 48
Smith, R 87
Smith, Wreford 101, 114
Smithson, S F 64
Solai 77, 78, 80, 84
Solai, Lake 82
Someren, Dr van 114
Sosiani River 101
Sotik 51, 95
Soy 103, 115
Speke, Mrs Albert 72
Speke brothers 72
Spring Valley 15, 18–19
Sprott, F H 24
Stanley Hotel 21, 34
Stewart, Bob 114
Stewart, Dr 44
Steyn, E L Snr 103
Suam River 114
Subukia 77, 78, 79, 81, 82, 84
Subukia River 78, 82
Swahili (language) 24, 33, 109
Swift, Randall 55, 57, 58
Swinton-Hume, Lt Col G A 103
Symes-Thompson, Maj 37

Tana River 52, 143
Tanganyika 114, 145
Tate, H R 143
Tate, Jack 21
Teleki, Count 77
Thego River 148
Theririka 52
Thika 51, 53, 54, 55, 57, 58, 73, 145
Thika River 55
Thika Tramway 38, 53
Thomson, Joseph 110, 137
Thomson's Falls (Nyahururu) 137, 140, 147, 151
Thorp, J K R 120, 150
Timau 51
Tinworth, Eric 135
Todd, J H S 104
Trans Nzoia 107, 108–109, 111, 115, 116
Treetops Hotel 143–144
Trench, Jim 152
Trench, Walter 95
Tsavo 108
Tumutumu 46
Turbo 97, 106
Turi 93
Twist, Capt T K 41
Twist, J K 41

Uasin Gishu (the Plateau) 97–98, 99, 101, 104, 106, 107

Uaso Nyiro River 137
Udall, Bob 38
Udall, Grace (Mrs Wilkinson) 16
Uganda 27, 32, 87, 106, 107, 108, 114, 115, 119
Uganda Railway 14, 111, 130
Ukambani (Kamba country) 108, 119
Ullmann family 104
Ulu 119
Uplands (Bacon Factory) 33, 149

Victoria, Lake 41, 45, 130
Vidal, Capt 129
Viljoen families 98

Waal, John de 98
Waal, Mrs de (Mrs Dreyer) 102
Wachira, Godwin 54
Wahu, Grace 46
Waitangi 36
Waiyaki, Chief 43, 44
Walker, E Sherbrooke 143–144
Walker-Munro 58
Walsh, John and Mary 70
Walshe, Anne 75
Wanjohi Valley 141
Ward, Maj H F 41
Watkins, Archie 27
Watkins, family 22–24
Watkins, Frank 78
Watson, Mr and Mrs Thomas 44–45
Webb, Billiam 39–40
Webster, Betty 113
White, Maj 138, 141
White Rhino Hotel 143, 145
White Rocks Farm 82, 83
Whitehouse, Sir George 15, 130
Williams, Mrs E 103
Williams, Mrs L 13
Williamson, R 85
Williamson, Mrs Vera 81
Wilson Airways 27–28
Wilson, Capt 109
Wilson, Florence 27–28
Wilson, Sir Frank 151
Wilson, Marjorie 89
Wilson, Mr 108
Wilson, Newton 21, 22
Wispers Farm 22–24
Wood, J R 36, 38
Wood T A 21
Wyndham, Mr 55

Zanzibar 28
Zanzibar, Sultan of 21
Zimbabwe 141
Zyl, van family 138